Driving the Enterprise to Sustainable Excellence

Driving the Enterprise to Sustainable Excellence

A Shingo Process Overview

Gerhard Plenert

A PRODUCTIVITY PRESS BOOK

First published 2021
by Routledge
600 Broken Sound Parkway #300, Boca Raton FL, 33487

and by Routledge
2 Park Square, Milton Park, Abingdon, Oxon, OX14 4RN

Routledge is an imprint of the Taylor & Francis Group, an informa business

ISBN: 9780367484019 (hbk)
ISBN: 9781003041849 (ebk)

Typeset in Minion
by Deanta Global Publishing Services, Chennai, India

Dedication

To the Love of My Life –

Renee Sangray Plenert

Who Keeps Trying to Drive Me to Excellence!!!

– Gerhard Plenert

Contents

Acknowledgments

To give credit where credit is due would require credit given to the Shingo Institute and a long list of individuals, companies, and universities that the institute has worked with through the years. The list is far too long to give everyone credit, but the author acknowledges a few specific individuals who were instrumental in the development of this book's material. Those most closely involved during his tenure at the Shingo Institute were Shaun Barker, Ken Snyder, and Rick Edgeman. A special thanks to the Jon M. Huntsman School of Business at Utah State University for providing the institute with a home and an environment to learn, flourish, and grow.

NOTE: The quotes for Shigeo Shingo come from the books *The Sayings of Shigeo Shingo; Key Strategies for Plant Improvement*, Productivity Press, Cambridge, Massachusetts, 1987, and *Shigeo Shingo; Kaizen and the Art of Creative Thinking*, Enna Products Corporation and PCS Press, Vancouver, Washington, 2007. The Shingo slides and quotes that come from Shinto are used with permission from the Shinto Institute.

About the Author

Dr. Gerhard Plenert, former Director of Executive Education at the Shingo Institute, has more than 25 years of professional experience in organizational transformations helping companies and government agencies strive for Enterprise Excellence by utilizing the Shingo Model to drive cultural transformations. Dr. Plenert is an internationally recognized expert in supply chain management; Lean/Six Sigma; IT, quality, and productivity tools; and in working with leading-edge planning and scheduling methods. He has literally "written the book" on leading-edge supply chain management concepts, such as finite capacity scheduling (FCS), advanced planning and scheduling (APS), and world-class management (WCM).

His experience includes significant initiatives with Genentech, Johnson & Johnson, Aerojet Rocketdyne, Shell, Aramco, Sony, Cisco, Microsoft, Seagate, NCR Corporation, Ritz-Carlton, the US Air Force, and numerous other branches of the US Department of Defense. In addition, Dr. Plenert has consulted with major manufacturing and distribution companies such as Hewlett-Packard, Black & Decker, Raytheon, Motorola, Applied Magnetics, Toyota, AT&T, IBM, and Kraft Foods. He has also been considered a corporate "guru" on supply chain management for Wipro, AMS, and Infosys, and a Lean/Six Sigma "guru" for the US Air Force and various additional consulting companies.

With 14 years of academic experience, Dr. Plenert has published over 150 articles and 23 books on Lean, supply chain strategy, operations management, and planning. He has also written MBA textbooks and operations planning books for the United Nations. Dr. Plenert's ideas and publications have been endorsed by people like Steven Covey and companies such as Motorola, AT&T, Black & Decker, and FedEx. His publications are viewable at www.gerhardplenert.com.

Dr. Plenert previously served as a tenured full professor at California State University, Chico; a professor at BYU, BYU–Hawaii, University of Malaysia, University of San Diego; and has been a visiting professor at numerous universities all over the world from Europe to Southeast Asia, Latin America, and Australia. He has earned degrees in math, physics, and German, and he holds an MBA and MA in international studies and a PhD in resource economics (oil and gas) and operations management. Dr. Plenert continues to serve as a Shingo educator and examiner.

> Unless someone like you cares a whole awful lot, nothing is going to get better. It's not.
>
> **Dr. Seuss**

Introduction

It has been said that there are basically two types of companies:

1. Those that are trying to achieve excellence
2. Those that are too busy fighting fires to be bothered with excellence

The question that each company needs to ask themselves is, "which one are they?"

Several years ago, Dr. Gerhard Plenert was involved in a project for the Texas Office of the Attorney General. This required working with 80 branch offices throughout the state and analyzing their performance. The environment was somewhat unique in that each office had two bosses, an office manager, and a lead attorney. Dr. Plenert would go to the offices one at a time and spend time there, analyzing flow, efficiencies, line balancing, employee satisfaction and participation, etc. Afterward, he would sit down with the two "bosses" and give them a report on the performance of their branch, along with recommendations. He discovered things like backlog of mail in someone's drawer that would exceed one year, work overlaps between employees, highly disruptive flows, and major redundancies.

The results were mixed. Some locations paid attention to the recommendations and implemented changes. Others ignored the recommendations, feeling that they were either too busy to be bothered or that they did not feel the recommendations had merit. Because of the mixed level of interest, the reports received about any performance changes were also mixed. One of the Dallas offices excitedly called Dr. Plenert two weeks after his visit. They congratulated him and informed him that they immediately implemented all of his recommendations, and in the two weeks they were able to triple their throughput. Is this an anomaly?

Another interesting case is the NASA Space Shuttle. Was it a failure or wasn't it? Originally the shuttle was to go into space several times a year. In the end, it was less than once a year, and sometimes, a couple of years between flights. The difference occurred in the safety checks that had to be performed between flights. Each manufacturer of a component was required to create a list of areas requiring inspection between flights. And each of the inspection sheets must be completed. Unfortunately, the inspections, in and of themselves, were a good thing. However, the redundancies were enormous, and each redundant test had to be performed separately for each inspection sheet. Doing an inspection one time in order to satisfy all the times the inspection was required wasn't acceptable, because the inspections were performed by different teams. The various inspections could require minutes to days to complete. The accumulative time required by all the redundant inspections increased the lead time between flights to the point where the space shuttle program was considered to be a failure in that it did not accomplish the desired number of trips each year. It could not be cost justified. You could say that quality killed the space shuttle program. But in reality, it was a lack of Enterprise Excellence.

An old Chinese proverb comes to mind, which says that it takes 10,000 people to make bread. In this example, you have the person who sells the bread, but behind that person is:

- the one who delivers the bread
- the one who bakes the bread
- the store that sells the grain
- the one who collects the ingredients
- the miller who mills the grain
- the farmer who grows the grain
- the farmer who milks the cow
- the toolmaker who makes the shovel
- the steel smith who makes the steel
- the carpenter who makes the handle
- the logger who cuts the tree
- the toolmaker who makes the saw
- the stonemason who cuts the grindstone
- the builder who builds the mill
- the seamstress who makes the uniforms
- the carver who makes the buttons
- the weaver who makes the cloth
- the weaver who makes the thread
- and so on!

From this example, we see why it takes 10,000 people to make a loaf of bread. And every one of these individuals is important in the overall process. No one is unimportant or insignificant in this supply chain. Everyone deserves the respect that their performance and participation deserve.

> 94% of problems in business are systems driven and only 6% are people driven.
>
> **Dr. W. Edwards Deming**

Countless organizations have, at one time or another, begun a "Lean journey" or they have implemented a continuous improvement initiative of some sort. At the foundation of these initiatives is a plethora of tools that seem to promise exciting new results. While many organizations may initially see significant improvements, far too many of these initiatives meet disappointing ends. Leaders quickly find that Lean tools such as Six Sigma, Jidoka, SMED, 5S, JIT, and quality circles are not independently capable of effecting a lasting change. There is an integrated synergy that occurs between these various tools built upon a set of eternal principals that creates an environment of lasting change. That is the topic of this book: How to create a *sustainable culture of continuous improvement.*

Years ago, the Shingo Institute set out on an extended study to determine the difference between short-lived successes and sustainable results. Over time, the institute noticed a common theme: the difference between successful and unsuccessful effort is centered on the ability of an organization to ingrain into its culture timeless and universal principles rather than rely on the superficial implementation of tools and programs. These findings are confirmed time and again by nearly three decades of assessing organizational culture and performance as part of the Shingo Prize process. Since 1988, Shingo examiners have witnessed firsthand how quickly tool-based organizations decline in their ability to sustain results. On the other hand, organizations that anchor their improvement initiatives to principles experience significantly different results. This is because principles help people understand the "why" behind the "how" and the "what."

To best illustrate these findings, the Shingo Institute developed the Shingo Model™ (Figure 0.1), the accompanying *Shingo Guiding Principles*, and the *Three Insights of Enterprise Excellence*™. The Shingo Institute offers a series of six workshops designed to help participants understand these principles and insights and to help them strive for excellence within their respective organizations.

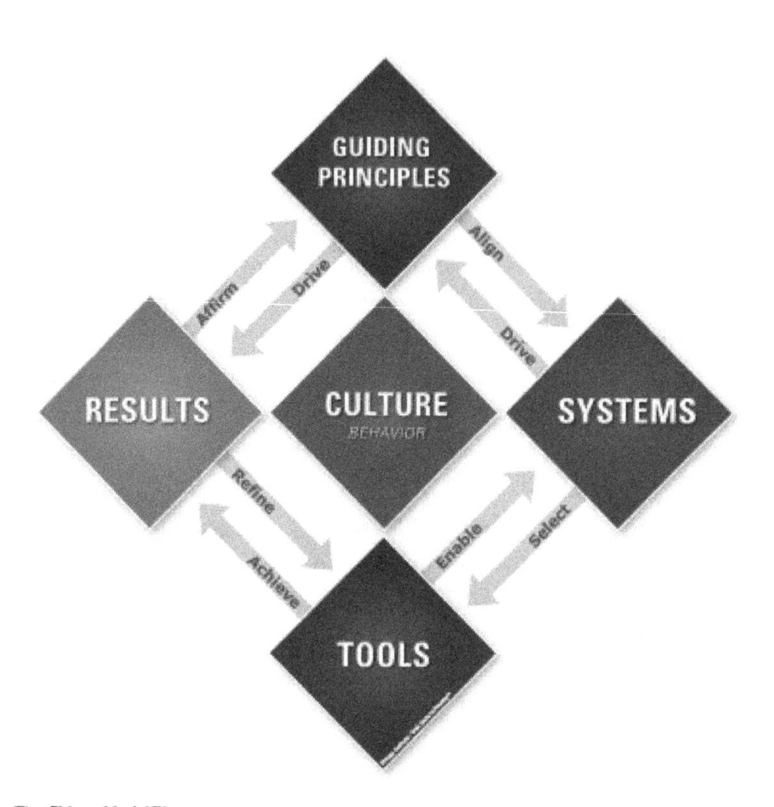

FIGURE 0.1
The Shingo Model.

This book is not a detailed review or a replacement of any of the Shingo workshops which teach in-depth the Shingo methodology far beyond what this book is capable of doing. This book is an overview of the entire Shingo process, starting with a discussion of the challenges that many of today's enterprises are experiencing. The author, in his role as a PhD in economics, has studied industries and has worked closely with many of them, attempting to understand their weaknesses. He has found that this is the only methodology which encompasses the Toyota Production System (TPS) principles at a depth and level that just studying the TPS tools can never accomplish.

Next, this book builds upon an understanding of these weaknesses. The book discusses how the overall Shingo methodology fits into these organizations and highlights the benefits. The next step is then to discuss what requirements are necessary for an organization to get ready for a Shingo transformation. What are the steps that the organization needs to go through, and when will it know that it is ready to begin?

This book briefly reviews the Shingo Insights and Principles (Figure 0.2) and explains how the Shingo courses should be best utilized to facilitate the desired transformation. It suggests some alternative plans for overall implementation based on the current state of the enterprise. It explains why there is no "one way" for successful implementation and how the implementation sequence needs to be customized to fit the requirements of each enterprise. It also discusses the length of time needed for success and how this differs depending on the current enterprise environment.

Lastly, the book explains how the implementation of a continuous improvement methodology and Shingo training for any enterprise is never finished. It is an ongoing process, and success is defined by internal improvements, not by some arbitrary external benchmark.

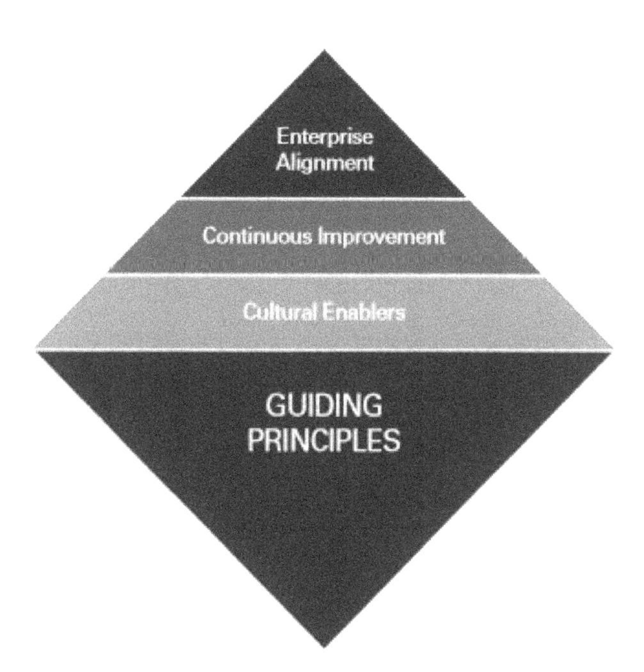

FIGURE 0.2
The Shingo Guiding Principles.

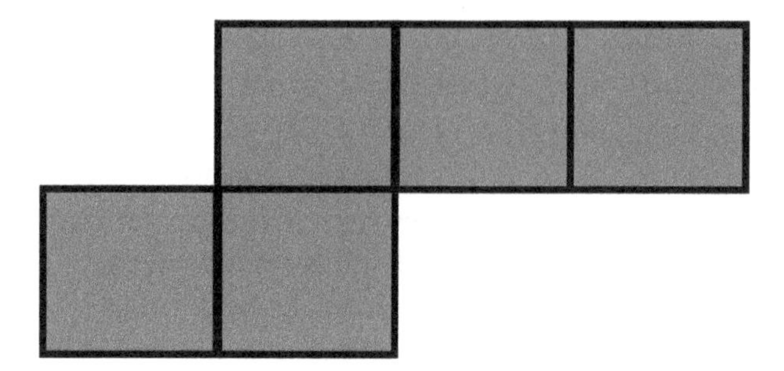

FIGURE 0.3
The Challenge.

The book is intended to be educational, thought provoking, entertaining in its stories and examples, and a guideline toward the development of a plan for continuous improvement. This book is filled with stories and examples, showing successful and not so successful implementations. The stories have been used to highlight many of the pitfalls that have arisen and may arise for the reader and which can be avoided if the reader is aware of them and knows how to watch out for them.

This book is filled with ideas intended to help the prospective Shingo implementor achieve success. Let's make you, the reader, successful.

But first, just for fun, one should look at how good our organization is at solving problems. Look at Figure 0.3. There are five small boxes. And the challenge is to change the five boxes so that by moving only two toothpicks you reduce the diagram so that there are only four boxes of the same size as each of the previous five. You have to reuse all the toothpicks, and you can't overlay them. (HINT: there are 16 toothpicks, and 4 boxes with 4 sides would require you to use all 16 with none of them being shared). The answer is hidden in later chapters in this book.

> It is not necessary to change. Survival is not mandatory.
>
> **Dr. W. Edwards Deming**

Part I

The Growth of the Shingo Approach

1

A Personal Experience

When I began visiting companies and production plants, there was one thing I almost always used to tell company presidents, "The medicine I am prescribing for you is a miracle drug and very powerful, but there is one problem with it."

"What problem?" they would say.

"The problem," I would explain, "is that the medicine won't work unless you take it. I may tell you wonderful things, but you're not going to be successful unless you actually do what I'm telling you."

Shigeo Shingo

THE STORY OF A DRIVE TO ENTERPRISE EXCELLENCE

The author has a personal experience which took a factory from confusion to excellence over a period of about 18 years. The company is TREMEC (Transmissions Y Equipos Mecanicos, S. A. – Mexican Division of Clark Equipment Co.) in Queretaro, Mexico, where he was employed in 1980 and 1981 as Manager of Corporate Organizations and Systems. He managed the design, development, and implementation of Corporate Manufacturing Control Systems and was responsible for all information flow equipment. This position had him working with employees throughout the facility, including all the far reaches of the production plant.

After his employment at TREMEC, the author earned two master's degrees and a PhD and went to work at a university, where publication of books and articles was critical. The author decided to write about his experiences at TREMEC, and these experiences were published in one of the premier production/operations management journals. In the first of these articles, "The Development of a Production System in Mexico," published in *Interfaces*, Vol. 20, No. 3, May–June 1990, pp. 14–23, the author gave the reader a frank and open case study of this 6,000 employee factory in Mexico. It discussed numerous problems with installing a production control system in this environment. It compared the Mexican process with a similar process in the United States. It then extrapolated and made suggestions for developing country installations in general. The full article can be found at https://pubsonline.informs.org/doi/abs/10.1287/inte.20.3.14 (Figure 1.1)

The article starts by saying,

> In designing and installing a manufacturing system for a factory in Mexico, we had to address problems and considerations that are typical in implementing production systems for developing countries; for example, the unskilled work force and poor power supplies. Other problems in planning and developing arose from conditions and goals that differ

FIGURE 1.1
TREMEC.

> from those in other developing countries; for example, poor employee-management relations. Many such problems can be avoided or solved with proper planning.

I will highlight several quotes from the lengthy article. These highlights demonstrate the struggles within TREMEC.

> "The upper management of the firm is composed of United States citizens; the secondary levels of management are primarily Mexican citizens trained or educated in the United States. Also, several United States advisors have been sent by the home office or by a United States automobile manufacturer." These advisors primarily acted like expeditors, trying to push product through the process.
>
> Most of the workers are unskilled: they have difficulty filling out time sheets. Most production was kept on schedule by chasing particular jobs around the plant in an attempt to get them done quickly. Although TREMEC has education programs with full-time instructors and classrooms, the need for more complete education for factory workers far exceeds the capacity of these education facilities.
>
> An adversarial relationship exists between top management and the heavily unionized labor force. The average unskilled worker resents his rich Mexican boss, who looks down on him. These workers also resent the Americans, who have to communicate with them through an interpreter, and who also make them feel inadequate.
>
> The average worker has a set of (personal) goals that are quite different than those of the company. He doesn't consider himself a part of the company, and he wants to spend as much time as possible with his family. This often means that after receiving a paycheck, he may not show up for work for several days. He'll return when he feels a financial necessity to go to work again.
>
> … production was scheduled using a computerized production control systems whose schedules were changed by the expeditors trying to push rush jobs through the plant. These altered schedules were then adjusted by the North American advisors … those schedules were overridden by top management.
>
> Middle management positions … are often filled through nepotism.
>
> Strikes occur frequently.
>
> Deliveries of raw materials are sporadic. … Therefore raw materials are heavily stockpiled.
>
> Equipment repair relies on scavenging for spare parts. … As a result, some of the machinery in the facility is usable only as a source for spare

> parts. … An enormous amount of scrap has accumulated due to obsolescence or to operational error. Gears that are several years old and red with rust are piled high in the yards.
>
> Production schedules are generated using unreliable standards. Much of the problem with the standards centers around the poor processes used to collect data. The employees recording production data do not understand its purpose and do not understand the procedures for recording information.

At this point, the article goes into detail discussing the implementation of on MRP II (Manufacturing Resources Planning) system (the early version of ERP – Enterprise Resources Planning). It discusses communications, technology, electrical power, data inadequacies, conversion, and training issues. Next, the article goes through each of the concerns with the TREMEC working environment and makes some recommendations. These major concerns are listed and include:

1. Unskilled work force – A recommendation for simplified input documents and input tools that do not require written information.
2. Unskilled middle management – Training on manufacturing production and control topics, including what metrics are critical.
3. Poor employee-management relations – Open sharing of information between all levels and helping them understand what the information is telling them.
4. Machinery that is too old, causing numerous breakdowns, or too technologically new and is therefore poorly understood – The recommendation here centers on a discussion about capacity management and safety machine capacity.
5. Poor power supplies – Power protection equipment and backup power systems.
6. Difficulty in (electronic) communications – This solution recommends a separate computer/technology center so that when a strike occurs, the entire facility is not shut down.
7. Poor or meaningless production standards – Improved data collection and manufacturing controls and efficiencies are recommended.
8. A crisis management mentality – Improving data and information will reduce tension.
9. High inventories – High inventories in raw materials, work in process, and finished goods need to be reduced and scrapped using tools like Lean's 5S program.

10. Poor routings – Improved data collection is critical.
11. Errors in data collection – Simplify the data collection process minimizing the need for writing and increasing the use of automated data collection where button pushing is all that is needed.

The article then goes into a discussion of the inadequacies of the MRP II (ERP) environment, like employee relations and employee management. It criticizes the use of US methodologies to motivate and inspire Mexican citizens, not recognizing the critical cultural differences between the two. It also criticizes the lack of culturally sensitive training in all areas of the facility.

The article summarizes some final thoughts on systems implementations that were relevant then and are still relevant today. Here is a summary of the "Final Thoughts" listed in this article:

1. "Any system that is not designed by a user will be only half effective." Systems should not be designed and implemented without the user's input.
2. "Save the manual system. If nothing else, the manual system can serve as a back-up system if the computer system fails." The two systems should mirror each other. There will be failures and shutdowns, but there should be logical workarounds.
3. "Never computerize something that doesn't work manually on a smaller and simpler scale. … The idea that changing a system instills discipline is false. Discipline is instilled by motivated management direction." The computer system should never complicate life. If it doesn't make things simpler for the user, the user will defeat it. Any time a system, computer or otherwise, doesn't make life easier for the user, it fails. Remember the saying that,

    No matter how good a system is, if it isn't easier to use than the previous system, and if the user isn't involved and own the system, it will fail. Similarly, no matter how poor a system is, if it's easier to use, and if the users have ownership in it, it will succeed!

4. "Choose a software system first, never the hardware."
5. "When considering the three phases of a system: input, process, and output, always analyze the output first and define the user's needs. Then analyze the required input to make sure the system's output requirements can be met."

6. "The systems analyst is generally wrong in any disagreement with the users. The users have to live with the system, so give them what they want."

It is important to note that the experience documented in this article occurred prior to the existence of the Shingo Institute, prior to the Shingo Principles, and prior to the Shingo Prize. The Shingo standard for excellence had not yet been developed. However, as the Shingo methodology developed, a transformation simultaneously occurred in TREMEC.

The author visited TREMEC between the publication of the first and the second articles, and the management of TREMEC was extremely upset with the author for the comments and concerns expressed in the first article. After visiting the plant the second time, the author published a second article, primarily focused on the changes and improvements that had already taken place within the facility. The updated article is "TREMEC Revisited: An Update on 'Developing a Production System in Mexico'" also published in *Interfaces*, Vol. 24, No. 6, November–December 1994, pp. 107–109. The full article can be found at https://pubsonline.informs.org/doi/10.1287/inte.24.6.107. This article was listed as an update on the changes that resulted since the previous article was published. This article was significantly shorter, only three pages long, and simply summarized some of the changes that have occurred up to the time of the article. Some significant highlights of the article include:

> In 1990, TREMEC, a transmission manufacturer in Mexico controlled by Clark Equipment, had many problems [Plenert 1990]. Since my previous article, many changes have taken place. These changes, many of which were brought about by the new Mexican-dominated ownership, have taken TREMEC out of the red and into the black.
>
> Today it produces transmissions primarily for the Mexican marketplace.
>
> Probably the most dramatic was that it (TREMEC) had separated itself from its previous United States influence. This immediately changed the management-to-employee relationships because it eliminated the United States "expert" who had tried to operate the plant in the same way that it would have been at home. The working atmosphere was more comfortable and less pressured. This is a move away from the crisis mentality that I mentioned in the previous article.
>
> Recently it has concentrated on quality and on cost reductions, primarily by reducing inventory. … It has implemented a more streamlined production flow that has reduced the work-in-process inventories by US $8 million.

> TREMEC is also experimenting with group technology manufacturing cells in an attempt to experiment with just-in-time (JIT) manufacturing philosophies. … The transfer to JIT seems to be moving along smoothly, more smoothly than similar transfers I have witnessed in the United States.
>
> Another major difference that I noted during my recent visit is the amount of training that the employees receive. … The lack of skill in the work force and in middle management has been greatly reduced by a new, stronger emphasis on training.
>
> Employee-management relations have been greatly improved by using local (Mexican) management and by eliminating United States advisors.
>
> Poor or meaningless production standards, poor routings, and error-filled data are all problems that have been eliminated as TREMEC has moved toward a materials-efficient system like JIT. … TREMEC now needs to collect a lot less data.
>
> The crisis management mentality seems to have been a United States management problem, not a Mexican management problem.
>
> Mexican companies, like TREMEC, have turned inward in their search for management talent, instead of looking to other countries, and they have found it to be plentiful.
>
> TREMEC's new management focus and new ownership has already taken the company out of the red and into the black.

As we can see from the time between the first and second articles, there has been an enormous transformation at TREMEC. But this was not the end of the story. TREMEC was then introduced to the Shingo methodology and incorporated it throughout their organization and, in 1998, applied for and was awarded the Shingo Prize for Operational Excellence. Here is a portion of the official announcement:

> **SHINGO PRIZE FOR EXCELLENCE IN MANUFACTURING WINNERS**
>
> LOGAN, Utah, May 5, 1998 – The seven companies (awarded the Shingo Prize) include two from Mexico, CYDSA IQUISA, Coatzacoalcos, and TREMEC, Queretaro. … TREMEC (Transmisiones y Equipos Mecanicos, S.A. de C.V.) produces transmissions for high performance automobiles such as Mustang, Camaro, Corvette, Viper and light trucks and military vehicles like Hummer and other automotive and agricultural vehicles for the American market. Employing over 1,800 people, TREMEC has increased sales per person by more than 83 percent in five years, increased

> the number of customers in 1996 by 60 percent and received General Motors 1996 and 1997 Supplier of the Year QSP award.
>
> **Ross E. Robson, Executive Director**
> Shingo Prize for Excellence in Manufacturing
> Utah State University
> Logan, UT 84322-3521

So what was this miracle road that, over an 18 year period, took TREMEC from a company swamped with inventory problems, operational problems, management–employee relationship problems, cultural problems, systems failures, etc. and allowed it to become one of the most excellently performing companies in the world. That's the journey and the story that this book will take us down – the road to sustainable Enterprise Excellence.

At this point, it would be appropriate to ask the question, "What is Enterprise Excellence?" The Shingo Institute asked some of the adherents to the Shingo process, and some Shingo Prize recipients, for their personal definitions of Enterprise Excellence. We asked, "What is Enterprise Excellence to you and your organization?" and here is how it was defined:

> Trying to instill purposeful change to mitigate the root cause of performance problems.
>
> Improving the work is the work. It is not just about doing the processes.
>
> Engaging the whole workforce and making a better company.
>
> Creating a great environment for the people, looking for the same objectives, and having fun everywhere.
>
> A status in which an organization has achieved not only financial or market results, but transcended to a different level where respectful people, culture, and principles are key factors in a strategy to sustain growth over generations.
>
> Understanding what customer needs are.
>
> Trying to optimize the value for customers.
>
> Being never satisfied. Constantly moving forward, constantly thinking.
>
> An organization where it's safe to challenge everything.
>
> A focus on culture and behaviors.
>
> One that enhances culture because it brings focus on the customer.

This book helps the reader understand the methodology that drives organizations toward building themselves into one of the world's best run enterprises.

The principle objective of management is to secure "maximum prosperity" for the employer and the employee. … The close, intimate, personal cooperation between management and men [employees] is the essence of modern scientific or task management. … When the elements of scientific management are used without the true philosophy of management, the results could be disastrous.

Frederick Taylor

REFERENCES (THESE REFERENCES ARE UTILIZED THROUGHOUT THE BOOK)

Hibino, Shozo, Kouichiro Noguchi, and Gerhard Plenert. *Toyota's Global Marketing Strategy: Innovation through Breakthrough Thinking and Kaizen*, Boca Raton, FL, Taylor and Francis Group, CRC Press, 2017.

Plenert, Gerhard. *Supply Chain Optimization through Segmentation and Analytics*, Boca Raton, FL, Taylor and Francis Group, CRC Press, 2014.

Plenert, Gerhard, Bill Kirchmier, and Gregory Quinn. *Finite Capacity Scheduling: Optimizing a Constrained Supply Chain*, Sacramento, CA, Self-Published, 2014.

Plenert, Gerhard, and Tom Cluley. *Driving Strategy to Execution Using Lean Six Sigma: A Framework for Creating High Performance Organizations*, New York, CRC Press, 2013.

Plenert, Gerhard. *Strategic Continuous Process Improvement: Which Quality Tools to Use, and When to Use Them*, New York, McGraw Hill, 2012.

Plenert, Gerhard. *Lean Management Principles for Information Technology*, Boca Raton, FL, Taylor and Francis Group, CRC Press, 2012.

Plenert, Gerhard. *Reinventing Lean; Introducing Lean Management Into the Supply Chain*, Amsterdam, The Netherlands, Elsevier Science, 2007.

Plenert, Gerhard. *International Operations Management*, Copenhagen, Copenhagen Business School Press, 2002 (republished in India by Ane Books, 2003).

Plenert, Gerhard. *The eManager: Value Chain Management in an eCommerce World*, Dublin, Blackhall Publishing, 2001.

Plenert, Gerhard, and Shozo Hibino. *Making Innovation Happen: Concept Management Through Integration*, DelRay Beach, FL, St. Lucie Press, 1997.

Plenert, Gerhard. *World Class Manager*, Rocklin, CA, Prima Publishing, 1995.

Plenert, Gerhard. TREMEC Revisited, *Interfaces*, Vol. 24, No. 6, 1994, pp. 107–109.

Plenert, Gerhard. *Plant Operations Deskbook*, Homewood, IL, Business 1 IRWIN, 1993.

Plenert, Gerhard. *International Management and Production Methods; Survival Techniques For Corporate America*, Blue Ridge Summit, PA, Tab Professional and Reference Books, 1990.

Plenert, Gerhard. The Development of a Production System in Mexico, *Interfaces*, Vol. 20, No. 3, 1990, pp. 14–23.

2

Who Is Shigeo Shingo?

In the final analysis, national prosperity depends on improved productivity and, conversely, it is only on a foundation of increased productivity that we can build a wealthy nation and happy citizens.

Shigeo Shingo

A TIME FOR REFLECTION

When Dr. Gerhard Plenert was traveling in Japan, working with his co-author on a different book, he would often join in with a group of academics and Toyota executives to discuss Toyota Production Systems principles. One night, during one of these discussions, the conversation turned to the United States. One executive stated, "Do you want to know what's wrong with the United States?" Unfortunately, this is a conversation that occurs far too often during international travels. Everyone seems to know what is wrong with the United States, and they are eager to share their insights on how to fix it.

Dr. Plenert was tempted to answer by saying, "Nothing! We are perfect. But I can tell you what's wrong with Japan." But instead, he did the courteous thing, trying to stay on their good side, and answered, "Tell me what you think is wrong with the US."

The executive came back with a very Lean answer. He suggested, "You're creating far too much non-value-added content."

Dr. Plenert responded with, "What does that mean?"

The executive drew a diagram on a piece of paper (Figure 2.1) as he said,

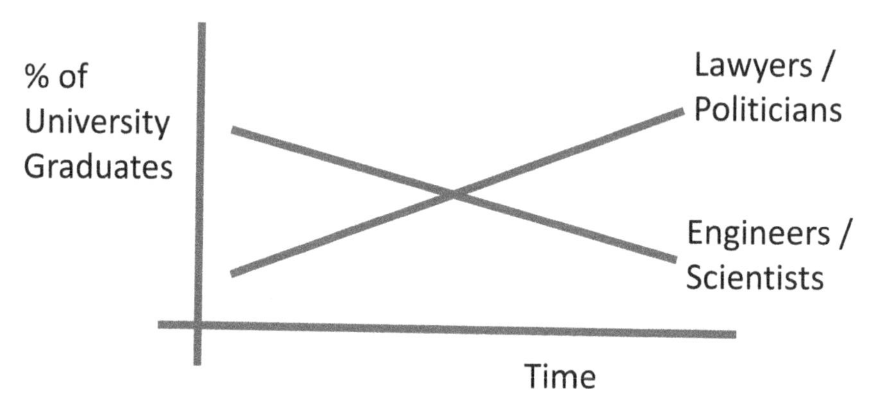

FIGURE 2.1
National Value-Added Content.

> Look at the students that you are graduating from your universities. You are graduating an ever-increasing number of non-value-added students and an ever-decreasing number of value-added students. The non-value-added students are using up resources, or at best just moving them around. But the overall value of the nation is not increasing in proportion to the size of the population. The United States is not producing enough resources to sustain its current standard of living in the long run. The value-added content is decreasing and so is the standard of living as a whole throughout the United States.

All Dr. Plenert could say was, "That's a very interesting perspective."

The executive ended with the comment,

> You need to shift the culture in the United States to be more focused on creating value. You need to change the way people think so that your students will want to enter into professions that grow the country, rather than just burn up its value-added content.

Dr. Plenert responded by smiling and saying, "I'll hurry back and tell our president what he needs to do to fix America."

"Excellent," was the executive's response. I think he seriously expected me to do exactly that.

The purpose of this story is to make you, the reader, think. Are we creating value as a nation? As a government (federal, state, and local)? As a company or agency? What do you, the reader, think? What about our culture? Is it based on principles? Is there a set of principles, like the Shingo

Principles that we'll discuss later in this book, that should be considered as a basis of principles for the nation as a whole? The point I am trying to make here is that the Shingo Guiding Principle structure is not just a structure for a factory or a hospital. It is a structure and methodology that needs to be applied at all levels, from the nation as a whole, down to the family or even the individual. The Shingo Principle methodology's usefulness extends far beyond what you will learn in this book. But for now, we need to have a starting point, and that starting point is you and your company. How can we make your enterprise excellent? But before we do that the author wants to take a pause, and in the next few chapters we will discuss:

- Who is Shigeo Shingo?
- What is the Shingo Institute?
- What is the Shingo Prize?
- What is the basis and birth of the Shingo approach?

SHIGEO SHINGO – A LITTLE HISTORY

In this chapter, I will attempt to briefly answer the question, "Who was Shigeo Shingo?" I will also answer, "Why is he important to continuous process improvement?" (Figure 2.2).

Shigeo Shingo (1909–1990) was born on January 8, 1909, in Saga, Japan, on the island of Kyushu. He first attended the Saga Technical High School and later studied at the Yamanashi Technical College in 1930, in the department of the Higher Technical School of Engineers in Saga, Japan, where he was impressed with the works of Frederick Taylor, an early American practitioner of operations management and process improvement. With this background, Shingo's career focused on industrial engineering, specializing in quality control. He is known for numerous quality concepts which became popular under the label of the Toyota Production System (TPS). These concepts included tools such as Poka-Yoke (Mistake Proofing), Single-Minute Exchange of Die (SMED), Just-in-Time Production, and Jidoka. His contributions to operations management and quality have significantly influenced Japanese and, more recently, Western manufacturing.

FIGURE 2.2
Shigeo Shingo.

Shingo's career started with working for the Taipei Railway Factory. Here he was responsible for measuring the efficiency of the production processes, including the employees. He observed that the production output was not maximized and that it did not run efficiently. Shingo decided to experiment with various incentives hoping to optimize production. His achievements at Taipei Railway Factory became the start of the many systems developments for which he is now famous.

Then, during World War II, the government sent him to the Amano manufacturing plant in Yokohama, where, as production manager, he increased productivity by 100%. In the mid-1940s until the mid-1950s, Shingo perfected many of his ideas for improving manufacturing efficiency.

In 1945, after World War II, Shigeo Shingo became a consultant for the Japanese Management Association. In this role, he taught various industries, like Mazda and Mitsubishi Heavy Industries, how to improve the management of their production processes. It was at this time that Taiichi Ohno, who is considered to be the father of the Toyota Production System, invited him to visit Toyota.

Shingo's involvement with Toyota started in 1955 when an engineer heard Shingo give a lecture. This was reported to Ohno, who decided to bring him in to speak at Toyota. Isao "Ike" Kato, a manager at the time with Toyota, coordinated a series of Shingo's visits over the next few years. It became Shingo's main focus to help Ohno and Toyota train manufacturing engineers in designing and implementing the efficiency processes Ohno had developed. These became known as the Toyota Production System. Shingo had introduced Toyota to a wealth of tools focused on process analysis, motion analysis, and time studies. He taught classes at Toyota, training thousands of Toyota engineers. He also developed the "P-Course" training program which assisted Toyota in its creation of Kaizen. As a result of his work at Toyota, Shigeo Shingo published the book *A Study of the Toyota Production System*.

Shigeo Shingo created a large number of quality control tools under the umbrella of the Toyota Production System (TPS), such as the Single-Minute Exchange of Die (SMED), which he originated in 1950. Shortly after that he also created the concept of Poka-Yoke in 1961.

Shingo's work and contribution were impressive, and it increased public awareness, resulting in his being awarded the Yellow Ribbon Medal in 1970. This award is given to individuals who have become public role models through their diligence and perseverance while engaging in their professional activities.

By 1977, Shigeo Shingo taught the world that in order to achieve zero defects in an operational process, it was crucial to take into account the human cultural aspect and its effects on the dynamics of the factory. This was the element that mechanical engineers had previously ignored and which he found critical.

Shingo's focus on the "human cultural aspect" is the piece that is often forgotten or even ignored when Westerners attempt to copy the Toyota Production System. Instead, they focus solely on the tools, and we will learn later in this book how inadequate focusing only on the tools can be. As you will see later in this book, the "human cultural aspect" is the heart of the Shingo methodology. It is this element that becomes the foundation of sustainable continuous improvement (CI) and Enterprise Excellence.

SHIGEO SHINGO – WESTERN INFLUENCE

Shigeo Shingo taught thousands of engineers at Toyota the Toyota Production System, influenced the creation of Kaizen, and developed his most impressive tool, the concept of the Single-Minute Exchange of Die

(SMED). However, in Japan, consultants are not given the same level of recognition as the employees, and therefore, many of his achievements were encased in the concept that became known as the Toyota Production System (TPS). The Shingo Institute, at Utah State University's Jon M. Huntsman School of Business, recognized Shingo's achievements, awarded Shigeo Shingo an honorary doctorate degree, and named the institute after him. The institute, following in Shingo's footsteps, focuses on educating organizational leaders worldwide about the tools and techniques that foster organizational excellence, using the Shingo Model based on Shingo's cultural transformation principles.

Shingo's ideas are encapsulated in his books and have had a revolutionary impact on Lean Six Sigma principles such as cutting waste, meeting customers' demands, making operations more efficient, and fostering a culture of continuous process improvement. Shingo has become more famous in the West than in Japan, partly because he wrote prolifically about process improvement and consulted with Western companies.

Shingo's instructional seminars at Toyota had a dramatic impact on the engineers' approach to process improvement. His books also had a similar impact on organizations outside of Toyota. Shingo had a knack for taking what was being done and stating it in logical terms. He was considered by many as not so much of an inventor as a person that could codify and rationally explain things in clear terms.

Although he was responsible for many creative tools, he is most remembered for his Single-Minute Exchange of Die (SMED) which has now become a Lean tool that is used to reduce the time it takes to change from running one process in an operation to making the shift to run a completely different operation. This reduces cycle time and costs while increasing flexibility. The "single-minute" is the goal of reducing the changeover time down to a time that can be measured in single-digit minutes.

Shigeo Shingo moved to the United States in 1980. At this time, Japanese cars had started to enter the American marketplace, and they outperformed their American counterparts, both in quality and in price. Shigeo Shingo was one of the few people living in the United States who understood the Japanese quality control system. Because of this, he had his book *A Study of the Toyota Production System* translated into English. This book was the introduction that popularized Japanese quality concepts which had been principally unknown in the United States up to this point.

Shigeo Shingo provided lectures, teaching and assisting American and European firms in the implementation of quality techniques in their manufacturing processes. He also wrote and published several additional books and papers on manufacturing.

Shigeo Shingo's work was now recognized in the United States and all over Europe, Asia, and Latin America. The Shingo Prize was created as a tribute to the efforts of Shigeo Shingo. The award is given to individuals that have achieved excellence in manufacturing, using his culturally transformative principles.

As stated in the *Shingo Model Handbook* published by the Shingo Institute:

> Few individuals have contributed more to the development of total quality management (TQM), just-in-time manufacturing (JIT), and Lean manufacturing as Shigeo Shingo. Many years before these ideas became popular in the western world, Dr. Shingo wrote about ensuring quality at the source, flowing value to customers, working with zero inventories, rapidly setting up machines through the system of "single-minute exchange of die" (SMED), and going to the actual workplace to grasp the true situation there ("going to gemba").
>
> Over the course of his life, Dr. Shingo wrote and published 18 books discussing these and other topics, seven of which have been translated from Japanese into English. He also worked extensively with Toyota executives, especially Mr. Taiichi Ohno, who collaborated with Dr. Shingo to apply these concepts.
>
> Always on the cutting edge of new ideas, Dr. Shingo envisioned collaborating with an organization to further his life's work through research, practical-yet-rigorous education, and a program for recognizing the best in organizational excellence throughout the world.
>
> In 1988, Dr. Shingo received an honorary Doctorate of Management from Utah State University in Logan, Utah, and later that year, his ambitions were realized when the Shingo Prize was organized and incorporated as part of the university.
>
> *The Shingo Model Handbook, Version 14.0*
> *© Copyright 2020, Utah State University*
> *The Shingo Institute, Pages 4 and 5*

> It is a universal truth that those who are not dissatisfied will never make any progress. Yet even if one feels dissatisfaction, it must not be diverted into complaining; it must be actively linked to improvement.
>
> **Shigeo Shingo**

REFERENCES

Hibino, Shozo, Kouichiro Noguchi, and Gerhard Plenert. *Toyota's Global Marketing Strategy: Innovation through Breakthrough Thinking and Kaizen*, Boca Raton, FL, Taylor and Francis Group, CRC Press, 2017.

Who Was Shigeo Shingo and Why Is He Important To Process Improvement? *Six Sigma Daily*, Retrieved 3/1/2020 from https://www.sixsigmadaily.com/who-was-shigeo-shingo-and-why-is-he-important-to-process-improvement/

Zeeman, A. *Shigeo Shingo*, 2018. Retrieved 3/1/2020 from ToolsHero: https://www.toolshero.com/toolsheroes/shigeo-shingo/

PUBLICATIONS AND BOOKS BY SHIGEO SHINGO ET AL.

The Sayings of Shigeo Shingo: Key Strategies for Plant Improvement, Boca Raton, FL, Routledge, 2017.

Quick Changeover for Operators: The SMED System, New York, NY, Productivity Press, 1996.

Construction of a Human Full-Length cDNA Bank, Gene, 1994, 1502, 243–250.

The Shingo Production Management System: Improving Process Functions Manufacturing & Production, New York, NY, Productivity Press, 1992.

A Study of the Toyota Production System: From an Industrial Engineering Viewpoint, Boca Raton, FL, CRC Press, 1989.

Non-Stock Production: The Shingo System of Continuous Improvement, Boca Raton, FL, CRC Press, 1988.

The Sayings of Shigeo Shingo Key Strategies for Plant Improvement, New York, NY, Productivity Press, 1987.

Zero Quality Control: Source Inspection and the Poka-Yoke System, Boca Raton, FL, CRC Press, 1986.

A Revolution in Manufacturing: the SMED System, Boca Raton, FL, CRC Press, 1985.

Study of "Toyota" Production System from Industrial Viewpoint, Japan Management Association, 1982.

The Toyota Production System, Japan Management Association, Tokyo, 1981, 52.

Fundamental Principles of Lean Manufacturing, Enna Products Corporation, Tokyo, 1977.

3

What Is the Shingo Institute and the Shingo Prize?

There are four purposes of improvement: easier, better, faster, and cheaper. These four goals appear in the order of priority.

Shigeo Shingo

MORE TO REFLECT ABOUT

We started the last chapter with a story about Dr. Plenert and his experience working with Toyota academics and executives. In a different, but similar conversation, the discussion in Japan focused on cultural shift and how you get people on board. The executives asked the question, "Where are the largest pockets of resistance to change? Who is the strongest in their resistance to a cultural shift?"

The academics, who had the most experience in teaching Toyota Principles, were quick to respond,

> There are three groups who give us the most trouble. They do not want to change. They like the status quo and want everything to stay just the way it is. They feel change is good for everyone else, but not for them. They become argumentative and try to find reasons why the changes they are being asked to make should not be made. Ironically, they are also the same individuals that are always pushing for everyone and everything else to change.

Dr. Plenert asked, "What are those three groups?"

The academics explained, "Doctors, Lawyers (which for them includes Politicians), and Academics."

What makes this conversation interesting is that these are indeed the groups that are always pushing for change and improvement. And yet they are found to have the most resistive cultures.

THE SHINGO INSTITUTE

The Shingo Institute (shingo.org) describes itself on the internet as a "not-for-profit organization housed at Utah State University and named after the world renowned Japanese industrial engineer Shigeo Shingo." The Shingo Institute describes its mission in two similar ways. The first, also from the internet, is that its role "is to guide leaders in creating sustainable cultures of excellence based on principles." The mission statement, as stated on their website, is:

> To improve the process of improvement by conducting cutting-edge research, providing relevant education, performing insightful organizational assessment, and recognizing organizations committed to achieving sustainable world-class results.
>
> https://shingo.org/

On this same web page, the Shingo Institute states its purpose as being:

> Based on timeless principles, we shape cultures that drive organizational and operational excellence.

The Shingo Institute is focused on honoring its namesake, Shigeo Shingo, remembering him for all his achievements in the areas of quality, productivity, and continuous improvement.

THE SHINGO INSTITUTE HISTORY

The Shingo Institute was founded to help companies across the globe strive to understand, embrace, and practice those successful Shingo concepts that date back to the original development of the Toyota Production System. The Shingo Institute is housed in the Jon M. Huntsman School of Business at Utah State University. It is also the home of the Shingo Prize, Shingo conferences and summits, Shingo workshops, and the Shingo Insight enterprise evaluation survey tool.

In 2008, after an intensive study regarding the necessary components of creating a company culture that can sustain improvements and consistently drive results, the Shingo Institute realized it needed to "raise the bar." The institute's attention shifted from an emphasis on a tool and programmatic assessment, primarily focused on operational excellence, toward the much needed complete assessment of the organization's culture as a whole, including all the interactions between the various functions of the organization and not just the operations areas.

While the Shingo Prize remains an integral part of the Shingo Institute, its scope has expanded to include educational offerings, an emphasis on new and innovative research and a growing international network of Shingo Institute Licensed Affiliates. Volunteer Shingo examiners, who are recognized as international experts in all aspects of Enterprise Excellence, visit organizations in order to evaluate the degree to which the *Shingo Guiding Principles* are evident in the behavior of all employees. They observe employee behavior and determine the frequency, duration, intensity, and scope of the desired principle-based behaviors. These examiners also observe the degree to which leaders are focused on these same principles and on culture, and the degree to which managers are focused on aligning systems that will drive ideal behaviors at all levels.

The focus at the Shingo Institute, empowered by its foundation on its ten principles, is unique in the world. The Shingo methodology is the most rigorous way to determine if an organization is fundamentally improving or just going through the motions of another flavor-of-the-month initiative. Using the philosophy and methodology of the Shingo Model (see Chart 3.1), the Shingo Prize has continued to evolve and strives to create its own brand of excellence based on the direction offered by Shigeo Shingo and the Toyota Production System. In 1989, the first Shingo Prize was awarded, and in 1993, in an effort to help companies achieve the prize, the clear structural definition of the Shingo Model was first developed.

In 2000, *Business Week* acclaimed the Shingo Prize as the "Nobel Prize for Manufacturing." Five years later, the first international Shingo conference was held in Mexico, affirming the Shingo Institute's international presence.

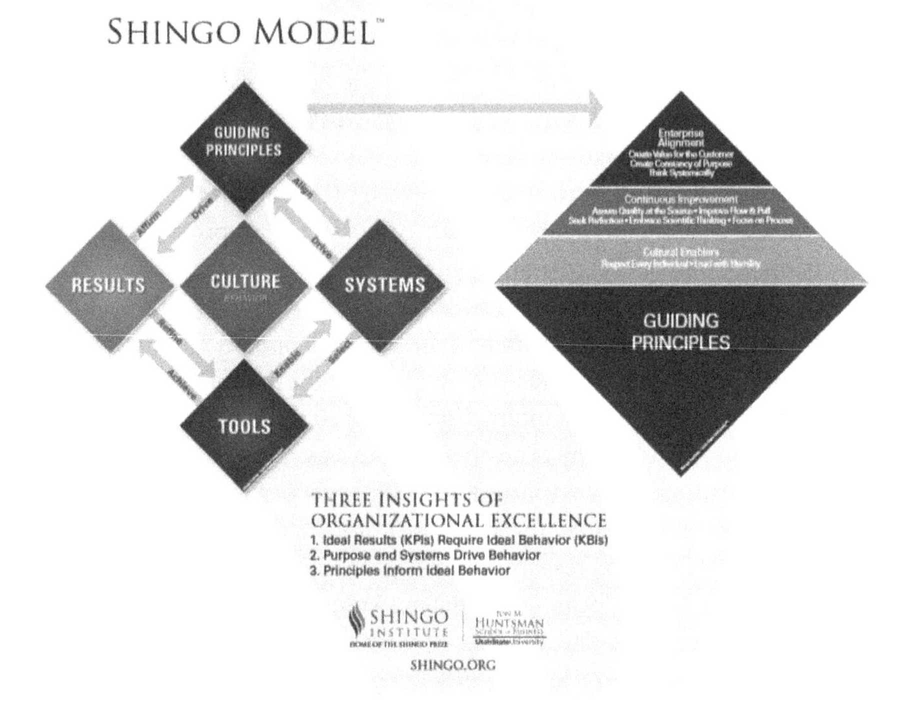

FIGURE 3.1
The Shingo Model.

With this growth came more improvements to the model and the prize until finally, in 2008, the Bronze and Silver Medallion categories were created. Today we find that many Shingo Prize recipients are household names like Ford Motor Company, Johnson Controls, Wiremold, Steelcase, E-Z-Go, Gulfstream, John Deere, US Synthetic, Goodyear, and Rexam, to name a few. A complete and updated list of the Shingo Prize recipients is available on the Shingo Institute website at http://shingo.org/awards.

DRIVING TOWARD ENTERPRISE EXCELLENCE

Initially, the famous Shingo Prize focused on operational tools and systems, and how utilizing those tools and systems drove results. The prize was given out based on results achieved using these tools. Unfortunately, far too many award-winning companies reverted back to their old ways. Tradition took over and the improvements were not sustained. The Shingo Institute realized there was a big piece missing from its earlier tool and system-based definition of Enterprise Excellence. It needed to be principle-based and needed to point toward a culture of sustainability.

In order to help enterprises create and identify sustainable improvement, the institute needed to make a cultural shift of its own methodology. It needed some continuous improvement of its own. It needed to stop focusing exclusively on tools and systems as the foundation for change, and instead embed strategies for continuous improvement that primarily focus on a cultural shift within the enterprise. Change is no longer something that happens once a year during a Lean event, after which the organization reverts back to its old ways. Instead, organizations need to imbed themselves in a culture where they are constantly looking for improvement opportunities. As Masaaki Imai says, the definition of kaizen is not just "continuous improvement," but rather, it should be "every-day improvement, every-body improvement, and every-where improvement." The cultural shift should be toward improvements on top of improvements and never reverting back to a traditional way of doing things.

In their quest to share their knowledge and insight with the rest of the world, the Shingo Institute developed, redeveloped, and continuously improved a model which has been the primary subject of their workshops (Figure 3.2). These materials were developed into workshops, which are continuously updated by the institute, specifically to share the knowledge of how to create a sustainable cultural shift which will ultimately lead to Enterprise Excellence.

THE SHINGO INSTITUTE: STILL STRIVING FOR ENTERPRISE EXCELLENCE

The Shingo Institute has developed a roadmap for those organizations that are striving for Enterprise Excellence. The journey starts with a series of six courses (Figure 3.2), teaching the basic concepts and principles of the Shingo Model and is organized in a way to help the enterprise build its own personal plan toward achieving excellence.

FIGURE 3.2
The Shingo Workshops.

The journey starts with a definition of what Enterprise Excellence means for your organization. These concepts are introduced in the first of these courses, the Discover Excellence (DE) workshop. DE is a foundational, two-day workshop that introduces the *Shingo Model*, the *Shingo Guiding Principles*, and the *Three Insights to Enterprise Excellence.* With real-time discussions and on-site learning at a host organization, this program is a highly interactive experience. It is designed to make the student's learning meaningful and immediately applicable as they learn how to release the latent potential in their organization and work toward achieving Enterprise Excellence.

There is also a *Discover Excellence* book authored by the same author, Gerhard Plenert, which outlines the basic concepts taught in this course. However, the Gemba "Go and Observe" experience, which is critical to understanding and delving deeply into these concepts, can only be experienced in the course.

The next workshop in the series that would be critical for a student to attend is the Systems Design (SD) course, which instructs the attendee on how to utilize and optimize systems so that they increase, rather than hinder, success. One of the key basic principles of any continuous improvement initiative is to create systems, and one of the foundational rules of all systems is to "Make the right thing easier to do than the wrong thing." Hence, the design of good systems becomes a work of art that requires extensive and close attention.

The next three courses each focus on the Shingo Principles. As you can see in Figure 3.1, there are ten principles, and these courses develop, in detail, the methodology and role of each of these principles. The first of these courses is Cultural Enablers (CE), followed by Continuous Improvement (CI), and last of all Enterprise Alignment (EA). These three courses can be taken in any sequence, but attending all three is critical before attending the last, capstone course.

CE builds upon the knowledge and experience gained at the Discover Excellence workshop and takes the student deeper into the Shingo Model by focusing on the two principles identified as Cultural Enablers: respect every individual and lead with humility. Cultural Enablers make it possible for people within the organization to engage in the transformation journey, progress in their understanding, and, ultimately, build a culture of Enterprise Excellence. This level of achievement cannot be accomplished through top-down directives or piecemeal implementation of tools. It requires a widespread commitment throughout the organization in order to be able to execute continuous improvement focused on the principles of Enterprise Excellence. This workshop is also interactive, with the first day spent in the classroom and the second day spent out "on the floor" where the student focuses on observing behaviors and identifying opportunities for improvement.

CI, the Shingo Institute's fourth workshop, begins by clearly defining value through the eyes of customers. It continues the discussion about ideal behaviors, fundamental beliefs, and behavioral benchmarks as they relate to the principles of continuous improvement. These principles are seek perfection, improve flow and pull, assure quality at the source, focus on process, and embrace scientific thinking. This workshop is also interactive, where each of its three days is spent in a blend of classroom and out "on the floor" Gemba activities.

The fifth workshop, EA, aims to help organizations develop management systems that align work and behaviors with principles and direction in ways that are simple, comprehensive, actionable, and standardized. The sum of individual efforts rarely approximates effective alignment of the pieces into a single integrated whole. Creating value for customers is ultimately accomplished through the effective alignment of every value stream in an organization. This workshop is the fifth of the Shingo workshops, diving into the principles of Enterprise Alignment which are Think Systemically and Create Constancy of Purpose. This workshop also examines results by looking at the related principle of Create Value for the Customer. Like the others, this workshop is also interactive with the first day spent in the classroom and the second day spent out "on the floor," observing behaviors and identifying opportunities for improvement.

Having completed the previous five courses, and not before all five have been completed, we are now ready for that capstone course, Build Excellence (BE). BE organizes and brings together the learnings from the previous five courses and assists the attendee in developing an integrated plan for overall success.

BE focuses on developing an executable plan for the enterprise-wide implementation of the *Shingo Guiding Principles*. This workshop addresses the integrated execution of systems that drive behavior toward the ideal as informed by the principles in the model. The Shingo Model (Figure 3.1) illustrates the relationship between tools, systems, principles, and results and explains how and why together they influence culture, which in turn produces results. This workshop answers the question: "How does my organization use the Shingo Model to transform its culture into one of continuously improving Enterprise Excellence?" This is not another program to implement; rather, it begins with the culture already in place and strengthens it by shifting behaviors to achieve improved results. With that said, the Shingo Institute recognizes that not all cultures are at the same stage in their progression toward Enterprise Excellence. This workshop helps build a customized, structured roadmap which is then used to execute cultural transformation built upon a foundation of principles, using tools that already exist within many organizations. It builds systems that drive behaviors to consistently deliver desired results. Build Excellence guides attendees through the development of an execution/deployment methodology that is customized to their organization's specific cultural needs and desired results. This workshop is also interactive, with the first day spent in the classroom and the second day spent out "on the floor" with a focus on observing behaviors and identifying opportunities for improvement.

The following are listed as the primary learning objectives in this final workshop as stated in the *Shingo Model Handbook*:

- Design or create an appropriate system, as taught in the second workshop and guided by the Shingo Model, which changes behaviors to close gaps. It should drive results closer to organizational goals and purpose.
- Answer the question, "How do I get everyone on board?"
- Understand the relationship between behaviors, systems, principles, and how they drive results.
- Learn how key behavioral indicators (KBIs) drive key performance indicators (KPIs), and how this leads to excellent results.
- Use the Gemba "Go and Observe" to understand the practical application of the *Shingo Guiding Principles.*

One thing that becomes obvious is that the attendee of the BE course has learned to define Enterprise Excellence very differently from when this same student attended DE for the first time. A cultural transformation has occurred. The following reflects some example responses from interviews performed by the Shingo Institute, where they asked some of the adherents to the Shingo process, and some Shingo Prize recipients, for their personal definitions of Enterprise Excellence. We asked, "What is Enterprise Excellence to you and your organization?" Here is how they defined it:

> Trying to instill purposeful change to mitigate the root cause of performance problems.
>
> Improving the work is the work. It is not just about doing the processes.
>
> Engaging the whole workforce and making a better company.
>
> Creating a great environment for the people, looking for the same objectives, and having fun everywhere.
>
> A status in which an organization has achieved not only financial or market results, but transcended to a different level where respectful people, culture, and principles are key factors in a strategy to sustain growth over generations.
>
> Understanding what customer needs are.
>
> Trying to optimize the value for customers.
>
> Being never satisfied. Constantly moving forward, constantly thinking.
>
> An organization where it's safe to challenge everything.

A focus on culture and behaviors.
One that enhances culture because it brings focus on the customer.

As you can see by these random definitions, the adherent to the Shingo process has experienced a cultural transformation. You do not hear anyone talking about profit, cost, and pushing the workforce harder. The comments you hear focus on enterprise culture and employee behaviors. These are the lessons learned during a study of and learning thoroughly about the Shingo methodology. That is what the Shingo Institute promotes, as can be seen in their earlier mission statements.

The Shingo Institute developed these courses but does not generally teach these courses. Rather it utilizes licensed affiliates, which improve the attendees' experience as they share their years of experience and a wide array of expertise to these workshops. These affiliates are located throughout the world and are available to support everyone on their journey, in whatever country or language. This localized expertise, along with specific local language considerations, is not available through the institute, which is the primary reason it uses affiliates. To learn more about each of the institute's affiliates, visit http://shingo.org/affiliates and contact the affiliate that best matches your needs. The public workshops offered by the Shingo Licensed Affiliates include the six shown in Figure 3.2. Currently, scheduled workshops can be found by contacting an affiliate in your area and one that speaks your language of choice.

Many organizations request privately held, in-house workshops, where the learning is specifically centered and focused on their internal issues and culture. The licensed affiliates listed on the website are often available to facilitate internal workshops specific to your organization and at your site. They would deliver Shingo education and, with years of consulting experience in various industries, can assist you with your specific challenges.

As there is far more to learn, discuss, and experience than one could ever manage to express and include in written form, the Shingo Institute invites the reader to further their education by exploring additional avenues of education. Beyond the workshops, the institute, and the licensed affiliates, the Shingo Institute offers publication recommendations and an internal assessment program which would help your enterprise determine where their weaknesses are and what their next steps plans should be toward Enterprise Excellence.

THE SHINGO PRIZE

The Shingo Prize is administered by the Shingo Institute. In addition to administering the Shingo Prize, the Shingo Institute creates and licenses educational workshops, organizes study tours, offers the Shingo Insight organizational self-assessment, and hosts annual conferences. The Shingo Prize is an award given to organizations worldwide by the Shingo Institute, a program of the Jon M. Huntsman School of Business at Utah State University in Logan, Utah. To be selected as a recipient or winner of the Shingo Prize, an organization "challenges" for the prize, meaning that they apply for the award. They are required to submit an achievement report that provides data about recent business improvements and accomplishments. If the enterprise passes this first level of assessment, then the organization undergoes an on-site assessment performed by Shingo Institute examiners. The focus of the on-site assessment is to confirm that the improvements cited in the report are prevalent throughout the enterprise. Organizations are scored relative to how they have demonstrated improvements and how closely their improvements match the ideal as defined by the Shingo Model™. Organizations that meet the criteria are then awarded the Shingo Prize. Two other award levels include the Shingo Silver Medallion and the Shingo Bronze Medallion. The Shingo Institute also offers the Shingo Research Award for academic publications and the Shingo Publication Award for relevant and successful practitioner-oriented books and articles.

In 1988, Utah State University conferred an honorary doctorate degree to Shigeo Shingo, the Japanese industrial engineer and author credited for his contribution of many of the principles, elements, theories, and tools associated with the Toyota Production System. That year, Utah State University established the North American Shingo Prize for Excellence in Manufacturing in Shingo's honor. At that time, the Shingo Prize for Excellence in Manufacturing was only awarded to organizations within the United States. Later, in 1994, Ford Electronics in Markham, Ontario, became the first international and the first Canadian organization to receive the award. In 1997, the award was given to the first Mexican organization, Industrias CYDSA Bayer.

From 2004 to 2008, a finalist category was added to recognize challengers that scored well in the evaluation criteria but did not meet the Shingo Prize level. This category was replaced in 2008 by the Silver and Bronze

Medallion awards. In 2008, Utah State University changed the name of the award to the Shingo Prize for Operational Excellence in order to reflect the altered criteria that broadened the award by making it available to organizations from all industries, not exclusively manufacturing. The focus of the award was also shifted away from recognizing only the use of lean manufacturing techniques based on the Toyota Production System (TPS) to recognizing the overall organizational performance in all aspects of the enterprise. The primary criteria became the existence of a cultural shift toward continuous improvement and moved away from simply a criteria based on the organization's utilization of TPS tools.

The Shingo Institute noticed that some of the recipients of the Shingo Prize prior to 2008 struggled to maintain performance improvements. They studied the differences between those who continued to improve and those who did not. Based on their research, the Shingo Institute created and published a new *Shingo Model* that focused on ten Guiding Principles to drive and sustain organizational improvement. Shingo examiners began assessing organizational performance based on the new principles rather than on the organization's use of lean manufacturing techniques and tools.

With the change in scoring criteria in 2008, the average number of organizations that received the Shingo Prize each year decreased from 11 to 2. In order to facilitate a continuing strive toward improvements, the Shingo Institute established the Shingo Silver Medallion and the Shingo Bronze Medallion award for challengers that scored well but did not meet the full standard and requirements of the Shingo Prize.

In 2009, Ultraframe in Clitheroe, Lancashire, UK, became the first European organization to receive a Shingo award, the Shingo Bronze Medallion. International interest has increased since that time. Nine of the eleven Shingo awards bestowed form 2014 through 2018 went to organizations outside of the United States. In 2011, Denver Health, Community Health Services received the Shingo Bronze Medallion, becoming the first healthcare organization to receive a Shingo award. In 2012, State Farm Insurance Operations Center in Bloomington, Illinois, received the Shingo Bronze Medallion, becoming the first financial organization to receive an award. In 2013, the division of Utah State University that administrated the Shingo Prize changed its name to the Shingo Institute.

As you can see from this history, the Shingo Prize has become the world's highest standard for Enterprise Excellence. As an effective way to benchmark progress toward Enterprise Excellence, organizations throughout the world may apply and challenge for this prize. Recipients receiving this recognition fall into three categories (taken directly from the *Shingo Model Handbook* which is available online at https://shingo.org/model/):

SHINGO BRONZE MEDALLION

The Shingo Bronze Medallion is awarded to organizations that are at the developmental stage as it relates to principles, systems, tools, and results. Behaviors and measures are identified, and the organization is working toward stability in both. Progress is made with respect to frequency, intensity, duration, scope, and role of the behaviors evident in the organizational culture.

Recent winners include:

2019 – Abbott Healthcare Products B.V., Weesp, Netherlands
Atlas Copco VT Service Center Technology Center, Cheonan, Korea
DSV Panalpina Sorocaba Facility, Sorocaba, Brazil
2018 – Cardiva Medical Inc., Sonora, México
Forest Tosara Limited, Dublin, Ireland
Ipsen Biopharm Ltd, Wrexham, United Kingdom
2017 – LEAR Corporation, Silao, Guanajuato, México
Cardinal Health, Quiroproductos de Cuauhtemoc, S. de R.L. de C.V. Cuauhtemoc, Chihuahua, México
Land Apparel S.A., Puerto Cortés, Honduras
Letterkenny Army Depot, PATRIOT Launcher New Build Program, Chambersburg, Pennsylvania, USA

SHINGO SILVER MEDALLION

The Shingo Silver Medallion is awarded to organizations that are well along the transformation path and heading in an appropriate direction as it relates to principles, systems, tools, and results. Behaviors and measures show results from a focus on key systems. Significant progress has been made with respect to frequency, intensity, duration, scope, and role of the behaviors evident in the organizational culture.

Recent winners include:

2019 – Analog Devices, Limerick, Ireland
Atlas Copco VT Service Technology Center, Jhunan, Taiwan
Boston Scientific, Clonmel, Ireland
Hologic Surgical Products, Coyol, Costa Rica
Visteon Electronics India Private Limited, Chennai, India
2018 – Ball Beverage Packaging Europe, Mont, Mont, France
Bridgestone BATO Shared Services Center, Heredia, Costa Rica
2017 – MassMutual, CFO and MMUS Operations, Springfield, Mass., USA
Visteon Electronics Tunisia, Bir El Bey Plant, Bir El Bey, Tunis, Tunisia

SHINGO PRIZE

The Shingo Prize is awarded to organizations that have robust key systems driving behavior close to ideal, as informed by the principles of organizational excellence, and supported by strong key performance indicator and key behavioral indicator trends and levels. Shingo Prize recipients show the greatest potential for sustainability as measured by the frequency, intensity, duration, scope, and role of the behaviors evident in the organizational culture.

Some recent winners include:

2019 – Abbott Nutrition Supply Chain, Sturgis, Michigan, USA
Abbott Nutrition Supply Chain, Singapore, Republic of Singapore
Boston Scientific, Coyol, Costa Rica
Merit Medical Systems Inc., Tijuana, México
Regeneron Pharmaceuticals Inc., Industrial Operations & Product Supply, Rensselaer, New York, USA

2018 – Abbott Nutrition Supply Chain, Granada, Spain
AbbVie Ballytivnan, Sligo, Ireland
Ball Beverage Packaging Europe, Naro-Fominsk Cans, Novaya Olkhovka, Russia
2017 – Abbott Nutrition Supply Chain, Sligo, Ireland
Thermo Fisher Scientific Baltics, Vilnius, Lithuania
Ball Beverage Packaging Europe, Naro-Fominsk Ends, Novaya Olkhovka, Russia

Organizations that are focused on the cultural transformation that the Shingo Model offers do not wait until they believe they might qualify for the Shingo Prize. Instead, they use the progression through the awards as a tool to guide their journey of continuous improvement. Some organizations that challenge for the prize do not intend to ever win the prize. They use the Shingo Model and the Prize Assessment process to measure their progression as they work themselves toward the highest standard of excellence in the world. They use the Shingo Principles as guidelines, which gives them direction toward achieving what they aspire to, and using these principles, they hold themselves accountable.

For most organizations, the desire to improve is instinctive. For an enterprise to be successful in the long term, it must relentlessly engage in a quest to improve. If an organization is to survive and thrive, its leaders must motivate their organization to be on a continuous pursuit of improvement. It is fundamentally impossible to achieve perfection because technology and other advances keep the target dynamic and always changing. However, the pursuit of it can bring out the very best in every organization and in every employee. Improvement is not easy and often not natural! It requires thoughtful leaders, smart managers with open minds, and empowered associates. Sustainable improvement cannot work under a "flavor-of-the-month" program or initiative. It requires a fundamental cultural shift which is enabled by the Shingo methodology.

Improvement requires more than the application of a new tool or a leader's charismatic personality. Excellent sustainable results require the transformation of a culture to one where every single person is engaged every day in making small, and from time-to-time large, changes. Every organization is naturally in some level of flux and transformation. The question we need to ask is, "Into what is the organization being transformed?"

The Shingo Institute has seen firsthand how some organizations have been able to sustain their improvement results, while far too many have experienced a decline. Years ago, the institute discovered a clear theme, "Sustainable results depend upon the degree to which an organization's culture is aligned to specific, guiding principles rather than relying solely on tools, programs, or initiatives."

The institute has developed the Shingo Model which will be referenced throughout this book, including the *Shingo Guiding Principles*. The Shingo Model provides a powerful framework that guides us in transforming an organization's culture and thereby focusing on and achieving ideal results.

Attempting to follow its own philosophies, the Shingo Institute has recently added two additional prize categories. The purpose of these categories is to encourage continuing research and publication that would foster new ideas and new methodologies that may, at some point, be adopted into the Shingo methodology. These two new awards are (Figure 3.3) (again taken from the *Shingo Model Handbook*):

PUBLICATION AWARD

The Shingo Publication Award recognizes and promotes writing that has had a significant impact and advances the body of knowledge regarding organizational excellence. Submissions for this award either contribute substantial new knowledge and understanding of organizational excellence or offer a significant extension of existing knowledge and understanding of organizational excellence. The types of accepted submissions include books or monographs, published articles, case studies, and applied publications/multimedia programs.

RESEARCH AWARD

The Shingo Research Award recognizes and promotes research and writing that advances the body of knowledge regarding organizational excellence. Submissions for this award either contribute substantial new knowledge and understanding of operational excellence or offer a significant extension of existing knowledge and understanding of operational excellence.

FIGURE 3.3
The Shingo Prize.

The types of accepted submissions include books or monographs, published articles, and case studies.

THE GUIDING PRINCIPLES OF THE SHINGO INSTITUTE AND THE SHINGO MODEL

The Shingo Institute continues to facilitate and educate the world on the process improvement principles taught by Shigeo Shingo. The ten principles that the institute utilizes, educates, and bases its awards on are the foundation that has made the Shingo Model so popular. These ten principles are briefly listed below and will be discussed individually and in more detail in a future chapter (Figure 3.4).

Respect every individual – This means treating everyone in an organization with respect and as a human being with potential. An

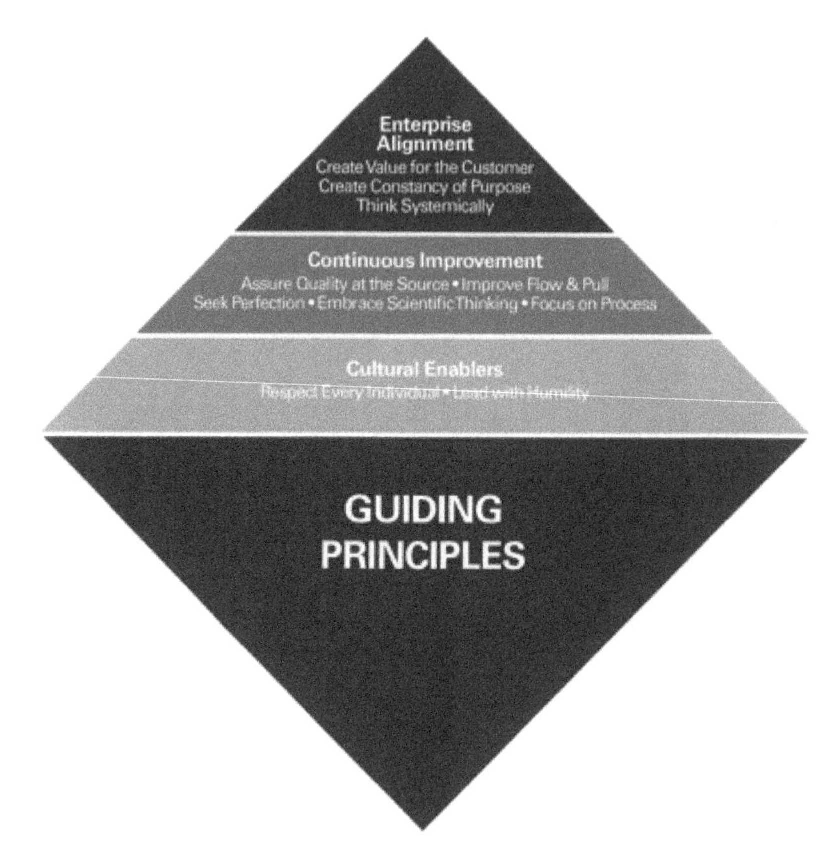

FIGURE 3.4
The Shingo Model Guiding Principles.

example of this would be creating an employee development plan that allows employees to maximize their potential.

Lead with humility – Leaders should seek input from others and always be willing to learn. Such leaders can create a culture where employees feel respected and energized.

Seek perfection – Perfection cannot ever be achieved, but the pursuit of perfection creates a culture of continuous improvement.

Embrace scientific thinking – Experimentation, observation, and a systematic exploration of ideas enable organizations to constantly improve and refine "our understanding of reality."

Focus on process – Every outcome is a function of a process. Understanding current processes and improving them leads to better outcomes. Problems usually involve processes, not people.

Assure quality at the source – Improved quality can only happen when every aspect of a process is done right the first time. Errors should be detected and corrected at the point of creation.

Improve flow and pull – Organizations create value for customers when they respond to real demand and create a continuous and uninterrupted flow. Anything that disrupts continuous flow is a waste.

Think systemically – Understanding every part of a process and how the parts interconnect can lead to better decision-making and improvements.

Create constancy of purpose – An organization's purpose and goals should be clearly communicated and understood by all. There needs to be "an unwavering clarity" on why the organization exists, where it is going, and how it will get there.

Create value for the customer – This is the foundation of everything. All value in an organization must be created by defining what a customer wants and what they are willing to pay for. Not doing so makes a company unsustainable.

SUMMARY

The Shingo Institute modeled itself on the principles of the world-renowned Japanese operations performance expert, Shigeo Shingo. Using his Toyota Production System tools, the Shingo Institute was able to Westernize the process by creating a model that incorporated those principles and teach enterprises how to ingrain them into their culture. This model is being used to develop a series of courses and training events, which include tours, conferences, books and newsletters, and a world of affiliates. The model and its principles helped to create and identify world class enterprises and reward them with the Shingo Prize, the ultimate measure of sustainable Enterprise Excellence. This book will now go on to expand on the Shingo methodology and demonstrate its success through a series of examples.

> Even the greatest idea can become meaningless in the rush to judgement. To gauge an idea as feasible we must cut our ties to the status quo and find the balance between constructive criticism and judgment. Within that balance we will uncover crucial input for making our ideas a reality.
>
> **Shigeo Shingo**

REFERENCES

Dillon, Andrew P., and Shigeo Shingo. *A Revolution in Manufacturing: The SMED System*, Boca Raton, FL, CRC Press, 1985.

Hibino, Shozo, Kouichiro Noguchi, and Gerhard Plenert. *Toyota's Global Marketing Strategy: Innovation through Breakthrough Thinking and Kaizen*, Boca Raton, FL, Taylor and Francis Group, CRC Press, 2017.

Plenert, Gerhard. *Supply Chain Optimization through Segmentation and Analytics*, Boca Raton, FL, Taylor and Francis Group, CRC Press, 2014.

Plenert, Gerhard, Bill Kirchmier, and Gregory Quinn. *Finite Capacity Scheduling: Optimizing a Constrained Supply Chain*, Sacramento, CA, Self-Published, 2014.

Plenert, Gerhard, and Tom Cluley. *Driving Strategy to Execution Using Lean Six Sigma: A Framework for Creating High Performance Organizations*, New York, CRC Press, 2013.

Plenert, Gerhard. *Strategic Continuous Process Improvement: Which Quality Tools to Use, and When to Use Them*, New York, McGraw Hill, 2012.

Plenert, Gerhard. *Lean Management Principles for Information Technology*, Boca Raton, FL, Taylor and Francis Group, CRC Press, 2012.

Plenert, Gerhard. *Reinventing Lean; Introducing Lean Management Into the Supply Chain*, Amsterdam, Netherlands, Elsevier Science, 2007.

Plenert, Gerhard. *International Operations Management*, Copenhagen, Copenhagen Business School Press, 2002 (republished in India by Ane Books, 2003).

Plenert, Gerhard. *The eManager: Value Chain Management in an eCommerce World*, Dublin, Blackhall Publishing, 2001.

Plenert, Gerhard, and Shozo Hibino. *Making Innovation Happen: Concept Management Through Integration*, DelRay Beach, FL, St. Lucie Press, 1997.

Plenert, Gerhard. *World Class Manager*, Rocklin, CA, Prima Publishing, 1995.

Plenert, Gerhard. *Plant Operations Deskbook*, Homewood, IL, Business 1 IRWIN, 1993.

Plenert, Gerhard. *International Management and Production Methods; Survival Techniques For Corporate America*, Blue Ridge Summit, PA, Tab Professional and Reference Books, 1990.

Shingo, Shigeo. *Fundamental Principles of Lean Manufacturing*, Bellingham, WA, Enna Products Corporation, 2009.

Shingō, Shigeo. *Kaizen and the Art of Creative Thinking: The Scientific Thinking Mechanism*, Bellingham, WA, Enna Products Corporation, 2007.

Shingo, Shigeo. *The Shingo Production Management System: Improving Process Functions*, Portland, OR, Productivity Press, 1992.

Shingo, Shigeo, and Andrew P. Dillon. *A Study of the Toyota Production System: From an Industrial Engineering Viewpoint*, Boca Raton, FL, CRC Press, 1989.

Shingo, Shigeo. *Zero Quality Control: Source Inspection and the Poka-Yoke System*, Boca Raton, FL, CRC Press, 1986.

Part II

The Shingo Methodology

4

Integrating the Shingo Methodology

No matter how effective it may be to set clear objectives and then strive to achieve them, bursts of effort alone won't do the trick; in the final analysis, methods must be improved.

Shigeo Shingo

MORE TO REFLECT ABOUT – AN EXAMPLE OF A WINNER (IN THEIR WORDS)

REXAM – Beverage Can South America – Águas Claras

Corporate overview: Rexam is a global consumer packaging company with a turnover of £4.9 billion in 2010. They employ some 22,000 people in more than 90 plants and offices in 20 countries around the globe. Headquartered in London, England, Rexam is an established member of the FTSE 100 (Financial Times Stock Exchange 100 Index), a global leader in the manufacturing of beverage cans and one of the world leaders in rigid plastic packaging. They are business partners to some of the world's most famous and successful consumer brands such as Coca-Cola, InBev, and PepsiCo, and blue chip global brand owners such as Proctor & Gamble and GlaxoSmithKline. Rexam's vision to "be the best global consumer packaging company" is strongly supported by Rexam's four embedded core values: continuous improvement, trust, teamwork, and recognition. They have been committed to a path of Lean Enterprise across all operations as a way of putting values into practice for over ten years. This approach is an essential part of what they call the "Rexam Way."

Continuous improvement process: Rexam has operated a global system of Lean Enterprise since 2004, structured around building capability in specific tool sets of culture, value stream mapping (VSM), 5S, total product maintenance (TPM), SMED, and Six Sigma. Progress is reviewed annually and awarded a merit of bronze, silver, or gold depending on performance levels. The Águas Claras plant achieved gold level at their first assessment in 2004 and consecutively in 2005, 2006, and 2007.

In 2008, Rexam's best plants were invited to participate in a more sophisticated assessment known as "Beyond Gold," where the implementation of Lean systems was appraised. Again, a system of merit is used to recognize achievements starting at emerald, then sapphire, and finally diamond. Águas Claras has ranked at diamond level since the first Beyond Gold protocol assessment was made.

Rexam has made more than 166 improvement implementations based on SMED and Kaizen methods since 2004, and value stream maps are revised twice a year, with the gap analysis resulting in a hopper list of main projects and actions linked to business goals.

They measure the effectiveness of actions and have increased from 73.2% in 2006 to 92% in 2010. The 5S program, introduced in 2004, involves all employees through internal audits with a robust management control system. The commitment to continuous improvement through Lean Enterprise has led Águas Claras to be the first Rexam Can site in South America to apply for the Shingo Prize.

The Águas Claras plant: The plant, based in the Brazilian state of Rio Grande do Sul, started operations in 2002. It is one of the 12 facilities that make up the manufacturing sector known as Beverage Can South America (BCSA).

Of the 111 people on site, 95 are involved in plant operations and management and 16 are responsible for logistics and distribution. The 167,000-sq.ft. facility has one aluminum can manufacturing line that is fully dedicated to customers such as Coca-Cola, Ambev, Schincariol, and Femsa, with a total production of 3.6 million cans a day. The plant operates 24 hours a day and 7 days a week, and the need for on-demand uptime drives a strong Lean culture. The plant's OEE (Overall Equipment Effectiveness) performance improved from 76% in 2004 to 85% in 2010.

The Águas Claras plant has an established decision-making culture based on Six Sigma analysis of manufacturing processes. The plant has been at the forefront of Rexam's Lean Enterprise success for many years now and is seen as a benchmark for other Rexam sites in South America and across the world to follow.

Product: The site is capable of producing two sizes of beverage cans, 12 oz. and 16 oz., for nine clients, resulting in over 101 active label options. The ability to continuously improve changeover times to meet smaller lot size requirements and make faster deliveries is at the heart of maintaining their competitive advantage.

To make a beverage can, the key process steps involve stamping and drawing aluminum discs from rolled stock to form a can shape. The cans are then washed before being labeled, using in-line screen printers. This plant was designed with a quality guarantee concept at every stage of the production process, without the need for final inspection for quality. Speed and quality are the key drivers of process performance, and our QAS (Quality Assurance System), RSVIEW (Rockwell Process Monitoring) system, and RSBizWare (Rockwell Database System) provide real-time production data and process monitoring capability.

ACHIEVEMENTS

Lean Enterprise Achievements

- Gold status 2004–2007, becoming the only plant to achieve gold status since the first year of assessment
- Beyond Gold diamond status 2008–2010
- Becoming the first plant in Rexam to win this certification
- Rexam's Best Lean Business in 2008
- Rexam BCSA Best Lean Enterprise 2010, Building a Winning Organization category
- Rexam People Development Award 2007 – For the excellence of the plant's programs in developing the skills and competencies of its team across the region
- PGQP (Local Quality and Productivity Program) achievements – Bronze level in 2004, Silver level in 2005
- ACIVI (Commercial and Industrial Association of Viamão City) – Silver Quality Award, 2005

- FEBRAMEC (Brazilian Fair of Mechanical and Industrial Automation) achievements – Awarded in 2008 for projects related to energy consumption and gas emissions. Repeat award in 2010 for the usage of the heat from oven exhaust chimneys in the can washing and water recycling process

Safety and Environmental

- ISO 14001:2004 Environmental accreditation OSHAS 18001:2007 Safety accreditation
- Rexam Risk Management Best Practice award for achieving best practice level in Health & Safety and Environmental categories, in 2005
- HACCP and GMP accreditation from the National Food Security Program in 2009 – Hazard Analysis and Critical Control Points, and Good Manufacturing Practices
- Annual safety training for all employees
- Monthly safety visits from management, covering all areas of operations, warehousing, and administrative areas
- "Elimination of Risk Points" program since 2006 has identified and treated more than 8,000 potential accidents and unsafe conditions
- Zero Lost Time Accidents since 2009
- Behavioral Based Safety program began in 2010 and has achieved a 100% rate of management engagement
- Zero Environmental Accidents since 2009

Quality

- ISO 9001:2008 Quality accreditation
- Assured quality through annual customer audits
- Two black belts (plant manager and TPM technician)
- Twenty-seven senior team members are green belts
- Another eight members of the senior team are training to be green belts
- QAS (Quality Assurance System) and QAS Minitab real-time SPC process monitoring covers 100% of production

Employee Morale

- Rexam is dedicated not only to people's quality of life, through a consolidated "Program of Wellbeing," but also to their career and personal development. All 111 employees at the plant are engaged in twice-yearly performance appraisals and objective setting, and 100% of people have had personal development plans since 2007
- Every quarter, the best employees are recognized for their engagement in all safety and Lean programs
- Plant "Good Day" program donates money to help social institutions, whenever safety, quality, and production records are achieved
- Annual events are held for all employees to discuss targets, process improvements, suggestions, and best manufacturing and administrative practices and to set up working groups to treat matters of engagement
- They invest in and stimulate a two-way open communication between employees and the leadership team, through constant alignment meetings, a suggestion program called "Open Channel" and other events
- Also, employees can count on established corporate communication channels, such as monthly newspapers, posters, special campaigns, and intranet news, to be informed of company guidelines
- Absenteeism rate of 1.52% since 2007

Delivery Performance and Cost Reductions

- OTIF (on time in full) performance has remained consistently above 85% since 2008
- Assured supply quality through annual audits with major suppliers
- Inventory turnover fell 11% since 2009
- Electricity consumption fell by 10% since 2007
- Thermal energy consumption fell by 12% since 2007
- Spoilage has reduced by 43% since 2003
- Over varnish usage fell by 22% since 2007
- LPG consumption fell by 6.5% since 2007
- Washer chemical consumption has reduced by 35% since 2006

This summary was written for Shingo by Jon Alder Director, Rexam Group Lean Enterprise.

MORE ABOUT THE SHINGO METHODOLOGY

The focus of this chapter is to give the reader a high-level overview of the Shingo process, the Shingo Institute, and the Shingo Prize. Far too many people touch only a small piece of the Shingo capabilities and never take full advantage of everything that is available. The Shingo Institute did not start out with a focus on changing the world of operations management through education. They started with the intention of challenging industry to follow the teachings of Shigeo Shingo and the Toyota Production System. The first Shingo Prize was awarded in 1989. The Shingo Institute (or Shingo Prize as it was initially called) fell into the trap of most of Western industry, looking for the one magical tool that would quickly convert Western inefficiencies and quality failures into a comparable Japanese model of success. The confusion of searching for that tool resulted in over 100 different tools being identified, the main ones being Lean, Six Sigma, TPS (TPS stands for the Toyota Production System but it is the Westernized version and not the actual process used by Toyota), Kaizen, Poka-Yoke, etc. From these tools, the first, early version of the Shingo Model was developed in 1993. It took several decades before industry and the Shingo Institute realized that tools, by themselves, will not create the transformations that the Shingo methodology is driving toward.

One Japanese Toyota executive was asked, "Why are you so willing to share all your secrets?" and the answer was, "By the time you figure out how to do this, we'll have innovated our process to the point where copying what we were doing decades ago will leave you decades behind what we are doing now." This has turned out to be very true.

The efforts of the Shingo Institute received US recognition for its effort to improve American industry. In 1994, the president of the United States recognized the Shingo Prize recipients. In 2000, *Business Week* magazine referred to the Shingo Prize as the "Nobel Prize for Manufacturing."

As the Shingo Institute realized that the winners of the Shingo Prize were often reverting to their old Western ways of doing things, they decided that they needed to review their focus on only tools and looked at the broader model, one that also focused on insights, principles, culture, and results. In 2008, a new Shingo Model was developed which incorporated these additional elements.

The Shingo Institute also realized that it wasn't enough to just evaluate companies based on their new model. They realized that they needed to share this knowledge, so that industry could understand how they were being evaluated. Companies were eager to learn how to become excellent. In support of this idea, in 2009, the Shingo Institute began the development of courses. Additionally, in an attempt to broaden their educational efforts, in 2010, the first Shingo International Conference was held.

The next big change for the Shingo Institute evolved around the realization that the Shingo Prize was not just for Americans. International companies from all corners of the earth were attending courses, attending conferences, and applying for the Shingo Prize. In 2011, we had more non-US applicants for the Shingo Prize than US applicants. There were numerous years where there were no American Shingo Prize winners; they all came from international locations. In 2015, the first Shingo Latin America Summit and the first Shingo European Summits were held.

This next big change also included the realization that the Shingo Prize was not just for manufacturing. Applicants and adherents came from sectors like health care, insurance, banks, international trade organizations, the military, and even governments. The first financial applicant was in 2012.

Obviously, the Shingo Institute drinks its own medicine and is a believer of continuous improvement, even for its own methodologies. At this point, let's return to a high-level discussion of the Shingo Model and how a follower of the Shingo methodology experiences the Shingo process.

LEARNING THE TOYOTA PRODUCTION SYSTEM (TPS) METHODOLOGY

There are two types of companies. The first is a company that is looking to improve. It knows that stagnancy and tradition will lead to failure. They are looking for changes and a change methodology that will make them more competitive.

The second type of company is one that feels they are too busy to waste time on changes. They are more worried about fighting fires and feel that if they put out the fires, they will be successful. As Shigeo Shingo would say, this type of company is doomed to bankruptcy. Without a methodology for continuous improvement, you cannot get better, and if you do not get better, your competition will run you over. Too many industries felt that they were untouchable, and now they are paying the price. Examples can be found in all industries. For example, NCR corporation thought that mechanical calculators would always be needed, until they were run over by IBM. Then IBM felt that small computers were not feasible until they were run over by Apple and Microsoft. Similarly, in the transportation industry, passenger rail travel felt that they would always be a permanent fixture for long distance travel until the airline industry ran over them. Tradition in industry is doomed to failure.

At this point, we will ignore the second type of company and focus only on the first, which is the one searching for a change. One thing that is certain in the changing world is that there are dozens and even hundreds of consultants out there who all have the perfect answer to what your company needs. All the big consulting companies like Infosys, Wipro, Accenture, and AMS have developed their own perfect models for change, and there are hundreds of books published on the subject. So where does a company go when they are in search of the perfect change model? Unfortunately, they typically end up trying several, failing with one, and then failing with another, spending years in their search. They may even have experimented with TPS, Lean, or Six Sigma and have failed because the changes that were identified and implemented did not stick in the long term.

Eventually, these companies encounter TPS, Lean, or Six Sigma tools like standard work, or 5S, or value stream mapping. They see spot improvements and are excited about what they see. But as one Hawaiian Coast Guard General once told the author, "I've had people implementing these tools for years and I still don't know if my over-all operations are any better." He experienced the spot improvements but wasn't sure if they stuck or if they were focused on the big picture of what the organization was attempting to achieve.

Seeing success in the TPS tools but not seeing sustainability or improvements of the big picture will turn the individual or company seeking for improvements to look for a reason for why these improvements are not sustained. That is when many of these searches turn to the Shingo Institute. The Shingo Institute offers a methodology that strives for change sustainability by integrating cultural changes with systems changes, with metrics changes, and with consistency.

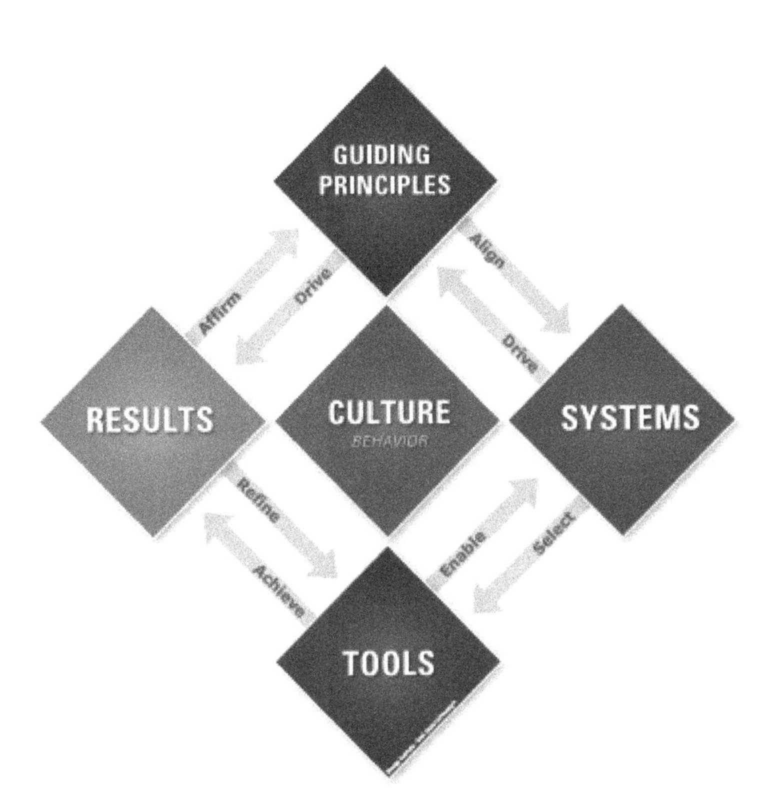

The *Shingo Model*™

FIGURE 4.1
The Shingo Model.

This chapter will give a high-level overview of how this integration occurs using Figure 4.1, which is the graphic for the Shingo Model. Future chapters will do a deeper dive into the methodology behind this model and how the integration process works.

CULTURAL SHIFT

As already mentioned, in 2008, the Shingo Institute updated its model (and it has been updated again and again over the years and will continue to be updated), and as of 2020, the model is the one seen in Figure 4.1. Follow your way around the model as I give a brief overview of how the model works in the remainder of this paragraph. Note that at the center of everything is culture. No matter how good the other elements are, like systems and tools, if the culture does not support the continuous improvement environment, tradition will kick in, and the culture will tend to revert to the equilibrium that the employees are familiar with and comfortable with. Therefore, in order to create the desired environment, the culture of the organization must be transformed. This transformation requires a structure of goals directed at the desired culture, supported by systems, which are driven by metrics that motivate a shift toward the desired culture and which encourage desirable behaviors. The redesign of the systems and metrics is where the tools come in. They are used to identify the systems transformations that are critical and the appropriate metrics which will support those systems.

It is easy to say that we need to use tools to redefine systems and then create metrics in support of these changed systems. Then, magically, we will have the cultural transformation that we are hoping for. The reality is that this is an enormous effort. It requires careful, detailed planning. The transformation happens over years. And it is not a one-time shot. The transformation occurs in stages. The most successful companies have experienced trials, failures, and numerous steps before they finally arrived at something that worked for them. And they are constantly tweaking and updating what they came up with. The journey is not quick and easy, but it is worth it, as you can tell by some of the success stories that are included in this book.

So where do we begin this critical cultural transformation? We start with defining who we are and what foundational "Guiding Principles" we want to use as the basis for our existence. These principles are the foundation upon which we build everything. Selecting these principles may already be transformational for our organization. They are universal and timeless, like motherhood and apple pie. They apply everywhere and always. The principles also need to be evident in that they are not invented, but rather they are discovered through research and study. Principles also govern consequences. Regardless of our understanding of the principle, when we act on it, we are subjected to the consequences of the principle, which are usually beyond our control. These Guiding Principles become the benchmark against which we validate everything else that we do.

> Principles always have natural consequences attached to them. There are positive consequences when we live in harmony with the principles. There are negative consequences when we ignore them.
>
> **Dr. Stephen R. Covey, author of the best-selling book**
> ***Seven Habits of Highly Effective People***

Guiding Principles define who we are as a company. They include Cultural Enablers, methodologies for continuous improvement, the top-to-bottom alignment of the enterprise, and creating value for the customer. These are foundational, unchanging, and constructively define the direction of the enterprise goals and continuous improvement process and highlight all the pieces that need to be transformed. Ultimately, the Guiding Principles (Figure 4.2) define the desired culture for the enterprise. The

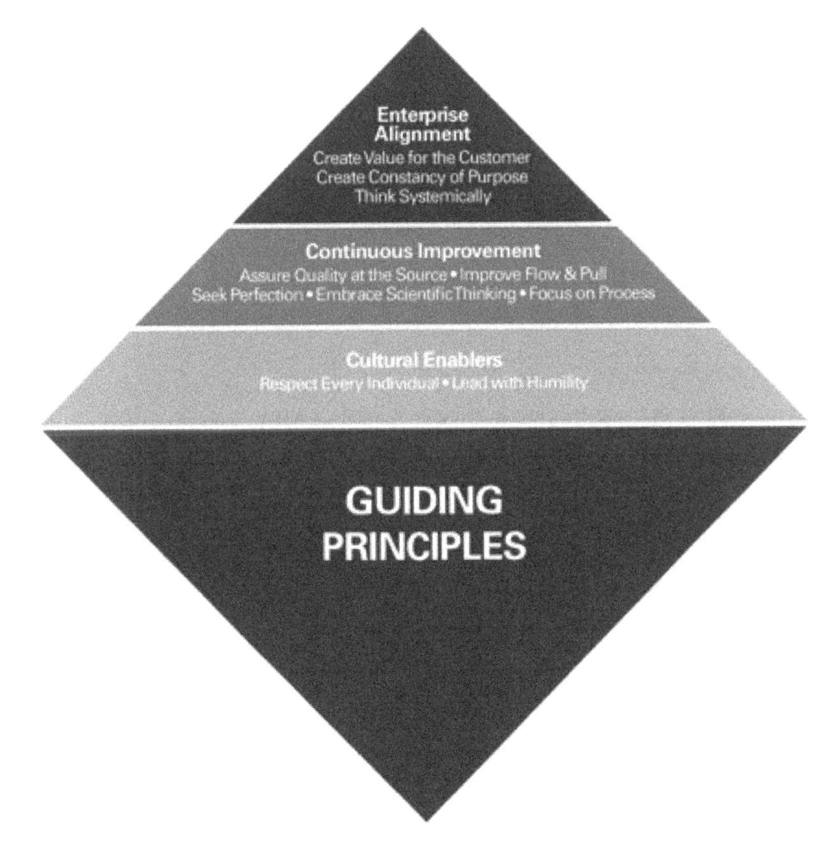

FIGURE 4.2
The Shingo Model Guiding Principles.

Shingo methodology walks the enterprise through the Guiding Principles as defined by the Shingo Institute and the enterprise would then adapt and customize those principles to fit the culture they want to ultimately achieve. Again, as in all the steps of this transformation, this is not an easy process. It takes time and extensive discussions, but once the principles for the enterprise are defined, they should be set in stone, and all other decisions should be built upon this bedrock foundation.

Next come the enterprise goals. What is it that the enterprise is attempting to achieve? If these goals are built upon the Guiding Principles, they will be structured very differently than previously. They will no longer be strictly financial. They will talk about topics like employees, customers, safety, and quality in a very specific way rather than using the generic verbiage like "Safety First" or "Satisfied Customer" that would have been used in the past.

But we are jumping ahead a little too quickly at this point. Let us talk a little more about the Shingo Insights that brought them to the realization that they needed a set of foundational Guiding Principles. We will do that over the next sections of this chapter. Then we will return to the other elements of the Shingo methodology, like results, systems, and tools.

Future chapters will do a deeper dive into everything that we discuss in this chapter, but for now, let us continue in this high-level overview of the Shingo methodology.

WHY ARE THERE THREE INSIGHTS AND WHY ARE THEY IMPORTANT?

The Shingo Organization, in unison with Shigeo Shingo and his son Ritsuo Shingo, and Dr. Stephen R. Covey and his son Stephen M. R. Covey, identified three transformation "insights" which aided in the defining of the Guiding Principle. The first of these insights is:

1. Ideal results require ideal behaviors – An organization's achievements are the result of employee behavior. If management goes through the hard work of developing Guiding Principles and creating a positive growth culture, employee behavior can be adjusted to achieve ideal results. Ideal behavior needs to become the expected behavior and needs to become evident in every team member.

2. Purpose and systems drive behavior – Beliefs define purpose, and purpose is used to define the systems that will then have a profound effect on employee behavior. What an employee believes in, and what they believe management believes in, is exhibited to them through the systems that each employee must work with every day. These systems affect what and how employees respond. For example, employees can make any metric look good if they believe that management thinks that the number is important to them, and especially if the employee feels that management evaluates employee performance based on that number. This connects directly to systems and measurements that the system incorporates. Most systems are designed to create a specific business result. However, far too often, the design of the system does not take into consideration the behavior that the system consequently drives. Management's ultimate job is to realign management, improvement, and work systems so that they drive the desired ideal behaviors. Ultimately, if this is correctly achieved, it drives the performance of all employees toward achieving ideal business results.
3. Principles inform ideal behavior – Principles, as we have already discussed, are foundational rules with consequences. They are the foundation that drives us toward ideal behaviors. The more deeply employees understand the Guiding Principles of an enterprise, the more clearly they understand ideal behaviors and can build systems which drive these behaviors and ultimately achieve ideal results.

The integration of these three insights explains how continuous improvement and striving toward excellence should work. It is not a onetime shot which places you on the road to success. It is a continuous revising of systems and metrics, based on the Guiding Principles, each time taking one more step closer toward those principles, and ultimately, as a byproduct of doing everything else correctly, allows you to the achieve the goals and results that your enterprise desires.

WHAT ARE THE CHARACTERISTICS OF PRINCIPLES AND WHY ARE THEY IMPORTANT?

According to Stephen R. Covey, a principle is a natural law that is universally understood, timeless in its meaning, and self-evident. Values govern actions, but principles govern the consequences of those actions. The Shingo Institute, in conjunction with Shigeo Shingo and his son Ritsuo Shingo, and Dr. Stephen R. Covey and his son Stephen M. R. Covey, identified ten principles that they consider to be the basis for building a sustainable culture which defines Enterprise Excellence. These principles are listed in Figure 4.2, where they are grouped into three categories, Cultural Enablers, Continuous Improvement, and Enterprise Alignment.

> There are three constants in live ... Change, choice, and principles.
>
> **Dr. Stephen R. Covey, author of the best-selling book *Seven Habits of Highly Effective People***

It is critical for an executive, leader, and manager to learn and understand these Guiding Principles thoroughly. Without having a thorough understanding, it is impossible to make decisions that support those principles. You cannot have a principle-based culture if you do not understand the principles. And once you understand them, you have just begun the arduous task of incorporating them into your organization through the development of meaningfully designed systems and metrics.

At this point, we should have an understanding of:

1. The integration and the need for a cultural transformation
2. The Guiding Principles which define the direction of this transformation
3. The enterprise goals (vision, mission, and strategy) based on the Guiding Principles and which target the desired, principle-based results
4. Metrics and systems which are principle based and which drive toward the goals
5. The need for tools that help to define appropriate systems and metrics

Reflecting back on Figure 4.1, we can take a closer look at the integration that was just defined. Let us look at each of the squares in the Shingo Model. For Guiding Principles, we see an arrow that indicates that Guiding Principles align systems, and in return, systems drive us toward the Guiding Principles. We also see that results affirm that our enterprise is correctly working itself toward the Guiding Principles in a way that we had hoped, while Guiding Principles should be the driving mechanism for those results.

Looking at tools, we see that the use of the proper tools both enables the proper design of focused systems and thereby assists in achieving the desired results. In the spirit of continuous improvement, results, good or bad, are the metric which identify the need for refinement through the use of appropriate tools, and continuous updating and revising of systems defines the proper selection of the tools that are needed to make appropriate revisions.

When executives and managers (leaders) understand Guiding Principles, they become empowered to take personal initiative. They want to teach employees (team members) those principles and how the tools that employees use support those principles. They understand how individual behavior can be pointed in the desired direction. They also understand the role that systems play in motivating ideal behaviors. And they understand the role that behavioral metrics, rather than performance metrics, play in creating a successful, sustainable environment (a detailed discussion about behavioral and performance metrics occurs in an upcoming chapter).

Future chapters will go through the Shingo Guiding Principles in detail. But before we do that, we will briefly discuss the importance of systems and metrics and the role they play.

SYSTEMS

> In spite of the fact that management is responsible for the system, or for lack of the system, I find in my experience that few people in industry know what constitutes a system.
>
> **W. Edwards Deming (1900–1993), American statistician who introduced quality control to the Japanese industry, author of *Out of the Crisis***

W. Edwards Deming describes a system as, "A system is a network of interdependent components that work together to try to accomplish the aim of the system. The aim of the system must be clear to everyone in the system."

Peter Senge, Senior Lecturer, MIT, and author of *The Fifth Discipline: The Art and Practice of the Learning Organization*, teaches the following about systems:

1. The word "system" is problematic. (It brings to mind computer systems and management control systems.)

2. A family is a good example of a system.
3. We live in interdependent webs of systems.
4. Systems complexity leads to problems that nobody wants.
5. We can solve systems problems by studying the interactions within the system. (Understanding the interactions will help us understand the cause of the problems and give us leverage to do something different.)

One fundamental truth about systems is that mistakes that occur in an operation are rarely the fault of the operator and usually the fault of a system's design inadequacy. Another truth that comes from TPS is that all systems should be designed such that the right thing is easier to do than the wrong thing.

From the *Shingo Model Handbook* we learn that,

> All work in an organization is the outcome of a system. Systems must be designed to produce a specific end goal, otherwise they evolve on their own. Systems create the conditions that cause people to behave in a certain way.

Poorly designed systems create bad behavior. Well-designed systems create consistent ideal behavior. It goes on to say, "When systems are properly aligned with principles, they strategically influence people's behavior toward that ideal."

A more detailed discussion about systems occurs in a future chapter. The explanation above is enough for this glimpse at the big picture of the Shingo methodology.

METRICS AND RESULTS

Employees at all levels can make any metric look good, if they think it is something their boss (which could be the board of directors or the shop floor superintendent) thinks is important. It becomes the responsibility of the boss, or leader, to make sure the employee is not misguided by having him or her working under the wrong metric. The metric should be focused on the goal of the system being used, which should, in turn, be focused on the goals and principles of the enterprise.

The journey toward excellence and continuously improving enterprises has traditionally focused on results, primarily key performance indicators (KPIs) like sales, revenue, stock price, or net profit. They achieve occasional spot improvement in their KPI results using a tool-based approach. This includes tools coming out of the Toyota Production System like value stream mapping (VSM), rapid improvement events (RIEs), and 5S. Additionally, they utilize continuous improvement strategies like Lean, Six Sigma (6σ), Theory of Constraints, Green, and many more. As stand-alone, these tools can provide spot results. But in order to achieve an environment of long-term, sustainable continuous improvement (CI) throughout the enterprise requires more than just tools. This book offers a thorough understanding of how excellent KPIs are simply the benefit of being an excellent enterprise, but they cannot be the goal.

So, what is our goal, if it's not KPIs? How do we achieve excellence? How do we define sustainable Enterprise Excellence as a measure of success? We need our business to take a slightly different perspective on how to achieve Enterprise Excellence. Instead of focusing solely on KPI results, we should instead consider behavioral elements that naturally drive us toward wanting to do the right things before we worry about doing things right. What if businesses focused on the relationships with and behaviors of customers, employees, suppliers, etc. instead of only KPIs? This is not to say that KPIs are not important. The Shingo Institute suggests that sustainable KPI improvement requires a cultural shift, or the improvement is only temporary. So how do we improve KPIs without focusing on KPIs? That is the subject of this book and the Shingo methodology.

In their search for improvement, most companies focus on tools that they hope will help them meet their goals. And the tools do offer spot improvements. The variety of tools along with the variety of solutions available is almost endless. Why then do enterprises struggle in sustaining their progress after reaching their fleeting KPI goals? Why do they fail to achieve Enterprise Excellence? To answer these questions, we need to first look at what has traditionally been their focus. As shown in Figure 4.3, the bridge toward sustainability requires more than just a pillar based on tools and focused on KPI results. Tools are important and they compose five of the ten Shingo Principles under the heading "Continuous Improvement" (refer back to Figure 4.2). But it is important to construct the second supporting pillar in order for the bridge to stay up. That second pillar is constructed based on the other five of the ten Shingo Principles under the

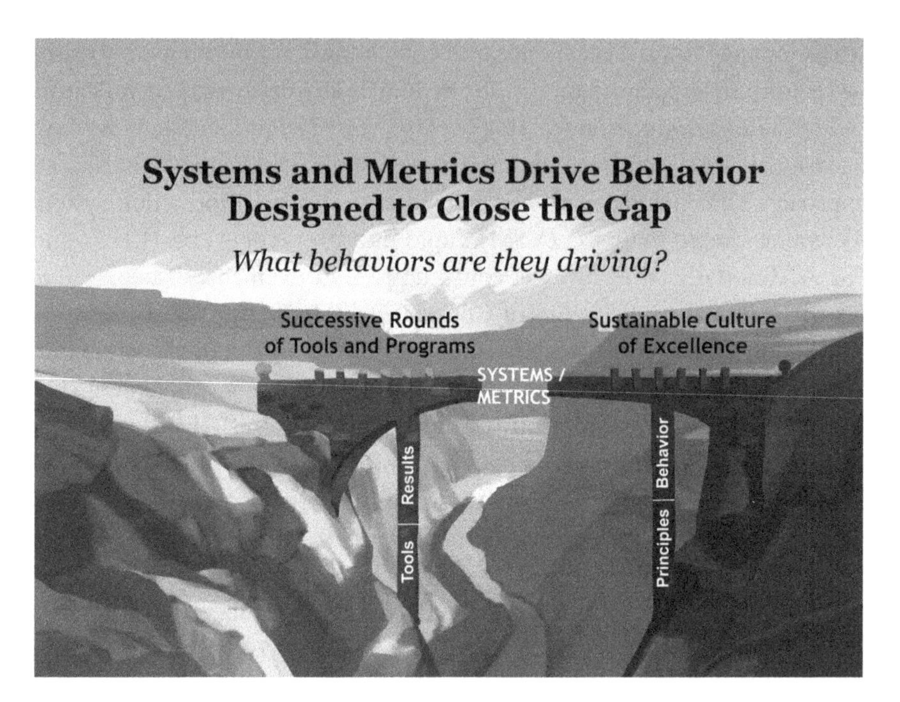

FIGURE 4.3
The Shingo Bridge to Success.

heading "Cultural Enablers" and "Enterprise Alignment" in Figure 4.2, as exhibited in Figure 4.4. Building these sustainable pillars and connecting both sides of the bridge together by bridging the gap between results (KPIs) and behaviors (KBIs) is the primary focus of the Shingo methodology and also the topic of this book.

Even though tools provide impressive results, the achievements are often fleeting and not long lasting. What we want to achieve is sustained superior performance, a sustained culture of excellence and innovation, and a sustained environment for social and ecological leadership.

The most widely used model in the world for this journey to Enterprise Excellence is called the Shingo Model™. It is based on the ten Guiding Principles in Figure 4.2 that are grouped into the three dimensions. The principles are timeless and universal. They apply to all cultures and nationalities and do not change over time. These principles provide a solid foundation for developing a roadmap to excellence.

Metrics and results comprise a complete future chapter. For now we will continue our overview by looking at tools.

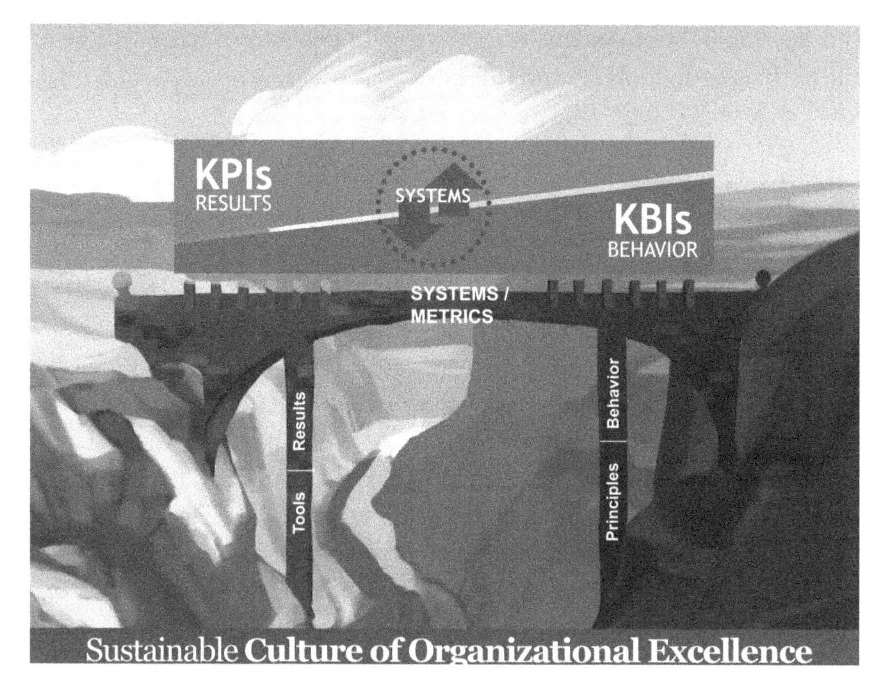

FIGURE 4.4
The Shingo Bridge to Success Using KBIs.

TOOLS

Reflecting back on the Shingo Model in Figure 4.1, we have covered all the elements of the model except the one on the bottom: Tools. Ironically, this is where most companies or employees start their journey toward what they hope will become sustainable continuous improvement. As listed in one of this author's other books titled *Strategic Continuous Process Improvement: Which Quality Tools to Use, and When to Use Them*, there are over 100 different "tools" that have been gleaned from TPS and from other sources, which all claim to be the perfect tool for continuous improvement. Obviously, they cannot all be perfect. However, many of them are the perfect tool for solving a specific type of problem. It becomes the job of the continuous improvement leader to know which tools fit which situation and what problems are best solved by each of the tools. The objective of the tools that are utilized should be to foster the growth and development of systems that drive ideal behaviors. There will be an entire chapter on tools later in this book.

CULTURAL SHIFT

Looking back on Figure 4.1, we are reminded that right at the heart of the Shingo methodology is the focus that we are driving toward something which is a cultural shift that will drive an organization toward excellence. Excellence is achieved by building an organization based on Guiding Principles, of which the Shingo Institute has offered its list of ten basic principles (Figure 4.2). These principles then become the foundation on which corporate goals are established (the left-hand box in the Shingo Model of Figure 4.1 labeled "Results"). A continuous improvement structure needs to be established which reviews and updates systems (the right-hand box), validating that they are based on the Guiding Principles. These systems are constantly reviewed and updated, making sure that they are using metrics based on key behavioral indicators (KBIs which come out of the "Results" box), which motivate employees toward ideal behaviors. KBIs, when designed correctly, will secondarily accomplish KPIs (also from the left-hand box). A plethora of tools exist, based primarily on TPS tools, which are used for the review of the organization's systems to make sure they are designed and focused properly.

That is it! That is the basic overview of the Shingo methodology. It is extremely powerful, and dozens of companies have found it to be the key to industrial transformations. The Shingo methodology is considered to be the international enterprise road to excellence. The next chapters will drill down on the various elements of the Shingo methodology that were introduced in this chapter.

> The most magnificent scheme in the world will be worthless if your perception of the current situation is in error.
>
> **Shigeo Shingo**

REFERENCES

Hibino, Shozo, Kouichiro Noguchi, and Gerhard Plenert. *Toyota's Global Marketing Strategy: Innovation through Breakthrough Thinking and Kaizen*, Boca Raton, FL, Taylor and Francis Group, CRC Press, 2017.

Plenert, Gerhard. *Strategic Continuous Process Improvement: Which Quality Tools to Use, and When to Use Them*, New York, McGraw Hill, 2012.

Plenert, Gerhard. *Lean Management Principles for Information Technology*, Boca Raton, FL, Taylor and Francis Group, CRC Press, 2012.

Plenert, Gerhard. *Reinventing Lean; Introducing Lean Management Into the Supply Chain*, Amsterdam, Netherlands, Elsevier Science, 2007.

Plenert, Gerhard, and Shozo Hibino. *Making Innovation Happen: Concept Management Through Integration*, DelRay Beach, FL, St. Lucie Press, 1997.

5

Systems

Improvement means the elimination of waste, and the most essential precondition for improvement is the proper pursuit of goals. We must not be mistaken, first of all, about what improvement means. The four goals of improvement must be to make things easier, better, faster, and cheaper.

Shigeo Shingo

MORE REFLECTION

The author of this book was brought into a factory that produced flexible electronics. It specialized in electroluminescence. This is a plastic product with circuitry painted onto the plastic. When attached to a battery and a small control module, it lights up, blinks, and has programmed effects. Its uses can be found in numerous car and truck dashboard displays. It can also be seen in signage, like in grocery stores and casinos, where electric sockets are not readily available.

The author was brought in as Director of Quality and was given the task of reducing their 13+% defect rate. Because of the high defect rate, the organization compensated by overproducing everything. And the financial losses had an enormous impact on their profitability.

Initially, the author became very concerned about the lack of direction within the organization. There was no strategy, vision, and mission statements which should be used to give the organization focus. There were no valid metrics, and it was impossible to say that the changes they made were strategically focused, because of that lack of direction.

The author started by insisting on a strategy workshop that needed to be attended by all senior management. In this two-day workshop, leadership and management were challenged to define the principles, goals, and direction of the organization. They were also challenged to create a New Product Development team, which previously did not exist. Without New Product Development, the author could not see a future for the company. And the author selfishly insisted that there be a focus on quality throughout all their messaging.

The next step was to define a set of metrics which could be used as a scorecard for measuring performance. These metrics would then be funneled down to the associate employees in a form that was relevant and specific to each of their functions and which gave them direction in their performance.

The strategy workshop was followed up with a series of workshops on tool training for all associates, primarily focused on the Continuous Improvement dimension of the Shingo Model. All associates were taught how to identify quality failures and how to make improvements. Everyone became responsible for quality.

At this point, the author was about five months into the organizational transformation because the various workshops took time to schedule. At this point, the author helped establish a "Quality Week," where the entire factory was effectively shut down, and the employees were instructed that they could change anything, move anything, fix anything, and position it anywhere in the plant. They had total freedom to make changes. But the rule that they had to live by was that "they could not produce one bad part." This, of course, threw leadership into a panic, but numerous previously failed attempts forced them to trust the process and they allowed "Quality Week" to move forward. Middle management was not convinced, but they were instructed to fall in line behind leadership on this initiative.

The cultural transformation had been put into motion, and, in spite of the resistance of middle management, it moved forward. The first day of "Quality Week" produced zero output. But an unlimited number of changes were made by teams of employees throughout the facility. The second day was a little better in that a few products were produced. By the third day the plant was at about 50% of its normal output. Surprisingly, by the fourth and fifth days, they exceeded their previous normal full day's output.

The culture of the organization had been irreversibly transformed. Employees felt trusted and empowered. In the future, if they wanted to fix something, they just went ahead and fixed it. If the change required funding, they went to the manager, and reasonable funding for improvements became commonplace.

The end result was that they no longer needed to overproduce in the way they previously were doing. In fact, they experienced about a 20% increase in capacity because they did not spend as much time producing bad parts or fixing product failures.

In the end, by the eighth month into his employment, when the author left this assignment, the defect rate was below 2%, and because of the cultural shift, the improvements continued, and it had continued to decrease and was less than 1% after 12 months. Inventory was dramatically reduced. Rush shipments were almost completely eliminated. And, in a surprising conclusion to the story, a buyer swooped in and made an offer for the company that the owners could not refuse.

What is the key message here? It is simply that the systems that existed did not support the company's goals (which also did not exist). There was no strategy system giving employees focus. There was no measurement system which gave employees direction. There was no training system teaching employees the basics of quality and continuous improvement. And there was no New Product Development system giving the company a future and longevity. The systems for this organization had to be rebuilt through a shocking transformation, and through these systems changes, the culture of the organization was able to be transformed.

SYSTEMS TRANSFORMATIONS

This chapter takes a large and significant step toward creating a plan that will drive us toward Enterprise Excellence. In order to take this step, we reflect back on the second of the three Shingo Insights from a previous chapter (Figure 5.1).

Purpose and Systems Drive Behavior

Using this insight, we focus on what a system is and how it influences behaviors. The systems that exist within an organization need also to fall in step with the enterprises' focus or goals. If the existing systems

Three Insights of Enterprise Excellence

1. Ideal Results Require Ideal Behavior
2. **Purpose and Systems Drive Behavior**
3. Principles Inform Ideal Behavior

Creating constancy of purpose.

Some points to remember:

1) Systems are interactive;
2) Systems can evolve over time to meet changing needs.

FIGURE 5.1
The Second Insight.

are not aligned, then tradition will dominate and take over. No matter how technologically good the system is, if it causes activities that are misaligned, it is a bad system. But instead of just throwing around the term "systems," let us identify some examples of systems that exist within your organization.

- Financial systems
  - Accounting
  - Payroll
  - Accounts payable
  - Accounts receivable
- Production
  - Production planning
  - Production scheduling
  - Materials planning
  - Materials forecasting
- Purchasing
  - Buyer systems
  - Procurement systems
  - Order processing
- Shipping

    - Routing systems
    - Sales order processing
    - Shipping schedules
    - Logistics
- Customer service
- Marketing
    - Sales forecasting
- Warehousing
    - Picking
    - Receiving
    - Lot tracking
- Maintenance

This list is by no means all inclusive. There are literally hundreds of systems and subsystems within any organization, and this list should cause the reader to identify dozens more that are not mentioned. This list should also allow the workshop attendee to realize that these systems are highly interrelated and connected to each other. Rarely is there a system that is not connected to, effected by, or has an effect on other systems. Systems are highly interactive, both with other systems and with their users.

Systems need to be flexible and evolutionary. They should never be declared as stagnant. We can never allow the excuse, "We've always done it that way" to become a standard operating procedure. Systems should always be dynamic. They should always be allowed to, and encouraged to, change.

At this point, we are going to take a step back and reflect on the teachings of an expert on systems. Russell L. Ackoff is a quality and systems guru who posted an interesting discussion of what a system looks like on YouTube, thereby putting it in the public domain. You are welcome to go to YouTube and view the actual video in its entirety. You will also be able to view the video during the Shingo systems workshop. The text of the piece of video that is relevant to our discussion of systems is as follows:

> Quality improvement is something that my principal mentor, Winnie the Pooh, called a good thing. Given that it's held so highly, it seems curious that in several national surveys recently conducted, over 2/3rds of managers

who would authorize the production quality and improvement programs considered those programs to be failures. Now the professionals tend to excuse that by saying the criteria for failure is irrelevant, it's not what we would have used. But that's irrelevant, because the definition of quality has to do with meeting or exceeding the expectations of the customer consumer. And the customer consumer is the one who authorized the introduction of the program. And therefore if their expectations are not met it's a failure, whatever the expectations. So it's important, I think, to understand why those failures have occurred given that quality of improvement are good things, so we can increase the batting average.

The hypothesis that I want to set forward to you is the reason for the failures is primarily the fact that they have not been embedded in systems thinking. They have been anti-systemic applications. Now let me try to explain what that means.

First what's a system? The system is a whole, spelled with a "w," that consists of parts, each of which can affect its behavior or its properties. You, for example, are a biological system called an organism. You consist of parts, your heart, your stomach, your pancreas, and so on. Each of which can affect your behavior or your properties. The second requirement is that each part of the system, when it affects the system, is dependent for its effect on some other part. In other words, the parts are interdependent. No part of the system or collection of parts have an independent effect. Therefore, the way the heart affects you depends on how the lungs are doing or the brain is doing. The parts all interconnect. Therefore, the system is a whole that cannot be divided into independent parts.

Now that has some very, very important implications that are generally overlooked. First, the essential or defining properties of any system are properties of the whole which none of its parts have. For example, very elementary systems you are familiar with are the automobile. The essential property of an automobile is that it can carry you from one place to another. No part of an automobile can do that. The wheel can't, the axel can't, the seat can't, the motor can't. The motor can't even carry itself from one place to another. But the automobile can.

You have certain characteristics, the most important of which is life. None of your parts live, you have life. You can write, your hand can't write. It's easy to demonstrate. Cut it off, put it on the table, and watch what it does. Nothing.

You can see your eye, can't see. You can think, your brain can't think. And therefore, when the system is taken apart it loses its essential properties. If I bring an automobile into this room and disassemble it, although every single part is in this room, I don't have an automobile. Because the system is not a sum of the behaviors of its parts; it's a product of their interactions. And that's been said here many ways, over and over today.

Now what does that mean? If we have a system of improvement that's directed at improving the parts taken separately, you can be absolutely sure that performance of the whole will not be improved. And that can be rigorously proven, but most applications to improvement programs are directed at improving the parts taken separately, not the whole. The proof is complex and I won't bore you with it.

Let's just take a simple example. I read in *The New York Times* recently that 457 automobiles are available in the United States. Let's buy one of each and bring them in a large garage. Let's then hire 200 of the best automotive engineers in the world and ask them to determine which car has the best engine. Suppose they come back and say, Rolls Royce has the best engine. Which one has the best transmission, we ask them. Come back and say the Mercedes does. Which one has the best battery? Come back and say the Buick does. And one by one for every part required for an automobile, they tell us which one is the best one available. Now we take that list, give it back to them, and say remove those parts from those cars and put them together for the best possible automobile. Of course, now we'll have an automobile consisting of all the best parts. What do we get? We don't even get an automobile. For the obvious reason, the parts don't fit.

Forms of a system depend on how the parts fit, not how they act separately. You see the architect, I think, understands systems best. They really have the fundamental idea.

When a client comes in and sees an architect and says, "I want to build a house for my family. Three bedrooms, family room, kitchen, two car garage. I want it all on one floor, I'd like it to be redwood, and I don't want it to cost more than $10,000 dollars." What does the architect do? He has a set of properties the client wants. Does he sit down and start to design the kitchen, and then the living room, and then the bedrooms, and then the garage? Is that what he does? Of course not. What he does is produce an overall design of the house. Now, he produces designs of the room to fit in to the design of the house, but he discovers in the process that he can modify the house in such a way to improve the quality of the rooms. But he will never modify the house to improve the quality of the rooms, unless the quality of the house is simultaneously improved. And that's fundamentally the principle that ought to be used in continuous improvement.

The second system principle that is ignored in most practices is that they practice in a way which derives from the work of Walter Shewhart in the Bell Telephone laboratories in the 1930s. Shewhart developed statistical techniques for determining defects. A defect is something that's wrong.

> Now this should be perfectly obvious: when you get rid of something you don't want, you don't necessarily get what you do want. So finding deficiencies and getting rid of them is not a way of improving performance of a system. That's easy to demonstrate.
>
> Take a television set. Go in and turn it on right now, what's the probability that you'll get a program you want? Well you probably haven't calculated it, but I have, .01%.
>
> Now it's a defect I can very easily get rid of. All I have to do is turn the channel. What's the probability I'll get a channel I want? Still .01 which means I have a 50/50 chance of getting a program I want even less. Basic principle, an improvement program must be directed at what you want, not at what you don't want. And determining what you want requires you redesigning the system. Not for the future but right now. And asking yourself, what would you do right now if you could do whatever you wanted to? Because if you don't know what you would do if you could do whatever you wanted to, how in the world can you know what you can do under constraints? But people don't ask themselves that question.

This full video is filled with excellent and inspiring perspectives on what a system is (it can be found at https://www.youtube.com/watch?v=OqEeIG8aPPk). Hopefully, you made notes during the video. From my perspective, some of the key points that Ackoff makes include:

- The failure to meet customer expectations results from anti-systemic thinking.
- A system is a whole – the sum of its parts.
- The parts of a system are interdependent and interconnected and cannot be divided into its parts and still function or accomplish what the system as a whole can accomplish.
- The essential or defining properties of any system are properties of the whole which none of its parts have.
- An improvement system that is directed at improving the parts taken separately may improve the performance of that part, but the performance of the whole will not be improved.
- An improvement program must be directed at what you want, not at what you do not want. Determining what you want requires you to redesign the system. Fixing a system defect will not fix the overall system.

What is a system?

1. A set of connected steps/activities/things/parts forming a complex whole.
2. A set of tools/procedures by which something is accomplished; an organized scheme or rules that governs behavior.

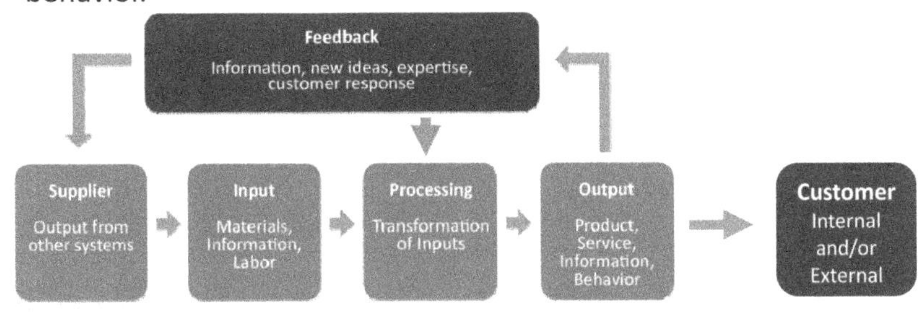

FIGURE 5.2
The System's Definition.

The last two items on this list are critical and extremely relevant to what the Shingo methodology is trying to accomplish. With this understanding of what a system is, we can now formulate a definition for what a system is. Our definition is (Figure 5.2):

> A system is a set of connected steps/activities/things/parts forming a complex whole. It is a set of tools/procedures by which something is accomplished; an organized scheme or rules that governs behavior.

If we take a careful look at the diagram in Figure 5.2, we should be struck by the fact that the boxes across the bottom are in the form of a SIPOC (Supplier – Input – Process – Output – Customer). These are all fundamental elements of a system. Another way of looking at this is that there is a source (supplier) of our inputs (input), which is then processed by the system (process), which causes a transformation of the inputs and creates a result (output), which is then turned over to the person receiving the results of the transformation or receiving the information created (customer). The performance, accuracy, and quality of the output generates a feedback loop back to the supplier of the inputs and

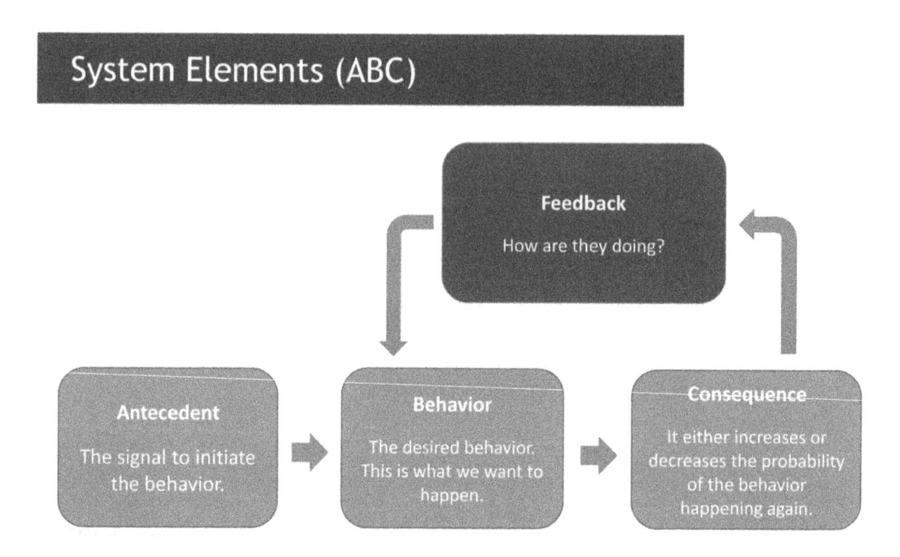

FIGURE 5.3
The System's Elements.

also to the process, which can then take any necessary corrective action to the current system or create new changes and transformations to the overall system.

Expanding on this foundational understanding of what a system is, we take the next step by understanding the ABCs of systems. In Figure 5.3, we see that the focus is on behaviors. We need to understand how the system effects behaviors. Only then can we start to think about if these behaviors are desirable, and, if they are not desirable, what type of systems transformation is necessary so that we can obtain the desired behaviors. In Figure 5.3, we see an Antecedent (the input, signal, or stimulus that triggers the behavior), the Behavior that is triggered and which is hopefully the desired behavior, and the Consequence which has the effect of causing a reoccurrence of the system or ending the use of the system. In case you did not get the message here, let me restate it in a different way,

> A system is triggered by input which causes a behavior. This behavior results in a consequence. If the consequence is aligned with the strategic objectives of the organization, then the system is a good system and its use will most likely be repeated. However, if the consequence does not align

> behind the enterprises' objectives, then the feedback mechanism informs the input that there is a need for a transformation of the system as a whole.

This is vital to understand the linkage between systems and behaviors.

Moving on to Figure 5.4, we see a graphic representation of the linkages and integration that occurs between systems. We also see how the behaviors that were triggered in one system become the inputs (Antecedent) of another or multiple systems. However, in each case, it is critical to validate that the output (Consequence) is aligned with the enterprises' strategic objectives. Ultimately, the highest level system, the corporate strategy system, also becomes the highest priority system.

The interconnectedness between systems should be understood and never sacrificed. Organizations that tend to silo themselves, either by departments or functions, sacrifice this interconnectedness. For example, the author has witnessed, in far too many cases, engineering departments that will have nothing to do with production. The engineers throw their designs over-the-wall to the production people, and if there are any failures in the design or its production, a long series of finger-pointing ensues. No one wants responsibility for any failures.

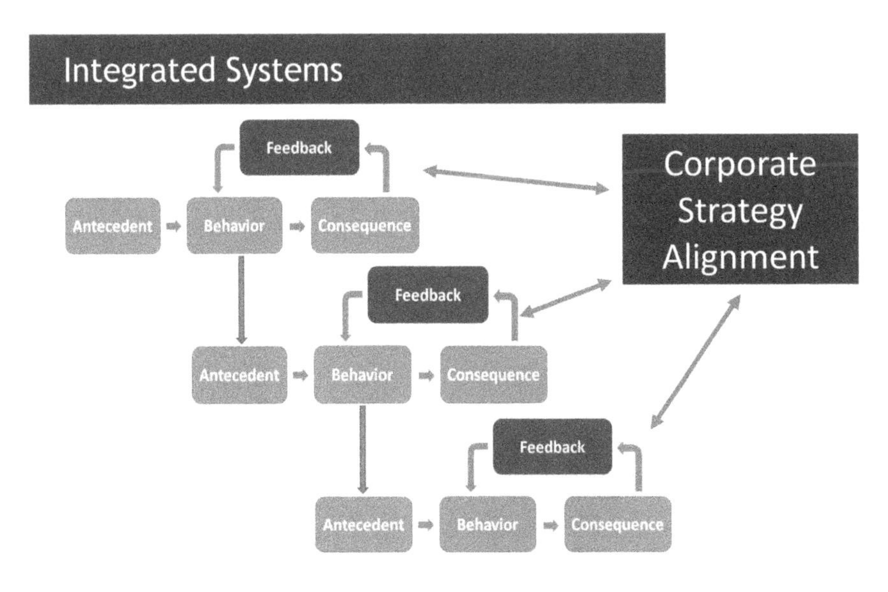

FIGURE 5.4
The System's Integration.

When NUMMI (the joint venture between Toyota and GM to produce cars and to learn from each other) was initiated, GM sent a large contingent of managers while Toyota sent engineers. Now, many years after the NUMMI experiment had ended, we can look around and see who learned the most from this experiment. GM resorted to tradition and is still doing the same things the same ways they have always done them, while Toyota has entered the US marketplace, set up factories throughout the country, and is producing Toyota vehicles with more American content than many of the vehicles that GM, Ford, or Chrysler are producing.

One lesson that we can learn from the Toyota Production System is that engineers need to come to the production floor and need to be involved in the production of the products they design. Often, engineers are required to produce the product for the first time. When this happens, we see examples like the table shown in Figure 5.5. Table A was the initial design by the engineers. They cut and folded a top. Then they cut and folded four legs, followed by cutting and folding eight braces. After all the cutting and folding, the braces, legs, and top were spot welded together (the black dots). The engineers, in conjunction with manufacturing, built the table, and they were very proud of their results. However, they made the mistake of asking manufacturing what they thought, and manufacturing suggested that they could make the entire table out of one sheet of metal and fold it together as shown in Table B. There would be no need for all the separate steps that Table A required, making 13 pieces, and would require the manufacture of only one piece. And the result would be a stronger, more stable table. Needless to say, engineering went back to the drawing board with their tails tucked between their legs. But this example is not intended to embarrass anyone. It is intended to show the need for interconnectedness when designing an integrated system (Figure 5.5).

At this point, it is useful to look at a specific example of how systems and behaviors are connected. To do this, while the author was still employed at the Shingo Institute as Director of Executive Education, he interviewed

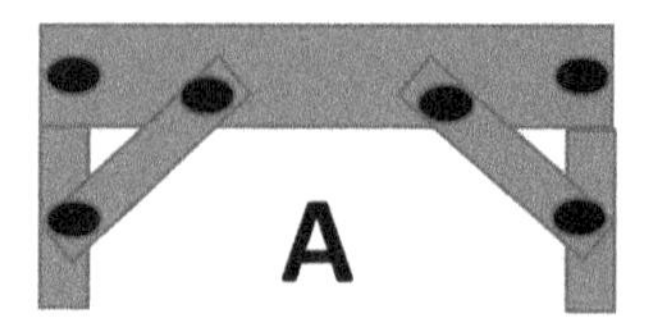

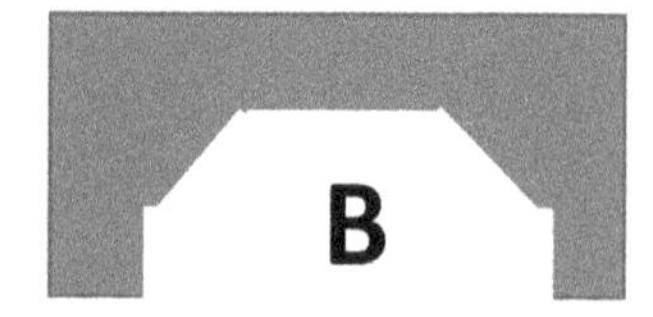

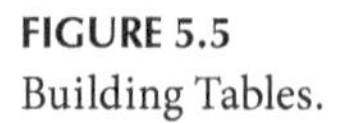
FIGURE 5.5
Building Tables.

a Shingo Prize recipient and had them discuss their experience. They used systems to modify behavior, each time validating that the changed behavior was, in fact, aligned with the corporate objectives. This interview will usually be presented as a video in the workshop, but here in the book, we will present it in text form. There are two individuals speaking, and their portions will be highlighted with their names at the start of each of their sections. They both work for OC Tanner Company, 1975 Main St, Salt Lake City, UT 84115. The interview was performed and recorded by the author of this book and is included in this book by written permission from Gary Peterson.

Gary Peterson, Executive VP, Manufacturing & Supply Chain
When we first began our lean journey 25 somewhat years ago, we had a situation where our culture was very tough and autocratic, very controlling. And people just did what they were told. Using their hands only, not really their brains. And as we tried to get them involved, our main experience was that they didn't feel like they had anything to contribute. We had effectively beaten out of them any sense that they could have impact. Any belief that they could help improve quality, that they could help the company become more efficient. In their minds, those were all things that management did. Not only is it management responsibility's but as an employee, I can't do anything about it.

So for us, it was important to change the mindset of our people. To help them start to realize, oh ok, I can have an impact on these important metrics. We decided that what we needed to do was change some of our systems to help people realize they could have an impact on the important metrics so one of the systems we used was our compensation system. Early on, we changed compensation so that people would understand that as they improved quality, as they improved efficiency, as they came to work and contributed to their team, they would get a raise. It wasn't intended as an incentive or reward it was more intended to align people to the outcome that we were seeking.

So we put in a weekly merit system, where every team and every individual had to qualify every week by hitting a quality rate, by coming to work, by being part of an effective team, by hitting efficiency and so forth. A team could qualify in a week but an individual might not qualify in a week. And each individual had to qualify fifteen weeks out of eighteen in order to get a raise. Initially, team members thought, oh you're trying to take away all future raises from us. You don't ever want us to get a raise again. They really didn't believe they could qualify in those fifteen weeks. But I remember fifteen, sixteen, seventeen some odd weeks into it, a team of the ring department got a raise and everyone was astonished. They were like, "how did they do that?" And the answer was that they solved their quality and efficiency issues. And fifteen, sixteen weeks later they got another raise and that really captured people's understanding. There were some other people who would just take on this victim mentality and thought this system isn't going to work for us. But once they saw other people using it, it was almost like a landslide. Teams said, "enough of this I'm going to go figure this out." And I really believe that within six to eight months, we had every team and every individual driving hard on the things that matter to us, on the metrics.

And it got to the point where it was the natural thing for teams and team members to receive the raises in a timely manner because they were driving the results that we wanted.

David Siebert, VP Customer Rewards Value Stream

Talk first again about compensation. I think with compensation your goal would be internally fair and externally competitive. That's the best you can hope for. You want employees to be happy but everyone wants more money. So it's a balance you try to obtain with compensation. You look at weekly merit, what happened with weekly merit is as leaders with team members began talking to them about their performance, what had happened is that leaders began to coach.

So when you change the culture like what we needed to do, the leader becomes someone different. And as you implement lean and people making improvements, the leader's got to be the coach not the go-to person. So as we implemented weekly merit, the leader would meet with the individual and determine if they made the week or not and in that process they begin to be a coach and the team member began to be an individual to drive improvements or make changes or do things in their power to make a difference, and that was a big deal to us. With weekly merit, as individual teams would work to obtain their goal, what happened is team members would learn to rely on each other. So it's not just about me anymore or my performance it's my team. So to make the week as a team, I have to help my team members. So that was a good turning point for us, and the team, as they begin to rely on each other in work.

Gary Peterson

Before we did the weekly merit system we had used the same semiannual raise for years and years. It was just a percentage increase for every person based on their current salary. This was our first attempt to do something different compensation. So we used this weekly merit system for about 3 years and it got to the point where everything was clicking, everything was humming. What we had a problem with at that point was cross training.

When we started our lean journey everyone did one job and it was the one thing they wanted to do. And they didn't want to learn to do a second thing. Which is very funny because now every employee knows more job skills than they can count. They not only move around with their own cell, they cut across value streams in the company. But at the time, everyone did one thing. And trying to get someone to learn a second skill was almost impossible, they just fought back. And so we decided at that point, let's align them to what we need which is multiple job skills and only pay as you learn new job skills. So the next way we changed our compensation system was to align people with job skills by saying as you learn these different job skills we'll give you a raise.

The impact of going to the job skills method was that some people immediately jumped on it and added a second, third, fourth job skill which was unprecedented for that time. But everybody learned that second job skill for the most part, many learned a third job skill. And they became more engaged and energized at the job skill process. After many years of the job skills process we actually had to put the brakes on it because everyone wanted to learn so many job skills we actually couldn't afford it. So we had people lined up in a queue to learn job skills. We did that for another 3 years so one day we were at a team meeting and talking about what's going on, what are you feeling, and the team said, "we need more job skills to be successful as a team."

We hadn't heard that before. Up to that point, we were saying "you need more job skills so the company can be more successful." Now we were hearing a team say, "if we had more job skills we could be more flexible, we could be more efficient, we could make good things happen." They wanted job skills and I was blown away by this revelation, by this change in what they were thinking. The system accomplished what we wanted it to do.

We explained to the team that, "fantastic, love the way you're thinking, we can only afford so much, so we have to kind of knead it out over a period time." And the team said, "well that's ridiculous, why don't we stop paying for job skills so we're not hampered by the pay?"

I couldn't believe it. I had a better gambling face on when they said it. I didn't look shocked, in disbelief. But I did ask them though, "Do you really mean that? Does everyone mean that? Are you saying that you want to learn job skills and you don't want us to pay you for that because the pay is in the way of you learning fast enough?"

And everyone was nodding, "absolutely, that's what we want."

This was just a few years after people did not want to learn a second job skill. So again I'm saying, this system worked. We said to them, "well let's walk around, let's visit some other teams, we'll tell them what you said, we'll see what they think."

We went to almost every team and when we said this other team said this everyone said "absolutely, we agree, get the job skill pay out of the way."

So in this case, they matured beyond the system. The system was no longer necessary to accomplish what we wanted, we were able to change to a new system.

So after the weekly merit, after the job skills pay, we kind of settled on more of the regular way of doing compensation. We settled on a standard raise where every employee got the same amount of money at raise time based on what the company could do.

For several years we paid a standard raise, it worked very well, kind of felt like we kind of landed on something that would last us for some time. But, some team members are working harder than others. Some team members are contributing more, and everybody on the team knows that. And we decided to change the system to allow for those who were the higher contributors to actually get a bigger raise.

So at that point, we began to rank our employees in each team based on contribution, top to bottom. And then we would put them on a graph of contribution compared to how much money they were making. Those people who were making less than market and who were high contributors, we accelerated them rapidly in their pay. People who were making more money but were maybe a regular contributor or a low contributor, and pulled them back in terms of their raise. So we had different levels of raise now based on contribution in the teams so high performers now were getting recognized through compensation and we're basically saying to everybody with this system that contribution matters. That your ability to give to the team makes a difference and we do recognize the high contributors and lesser contributors.

David Siebert

I think it's important to understand that as we did this contribution evolution, I would call it I guess, years of service didn't equal contribution. It's really about contribution and we define contribution as do things right, doing the right things, and influencing. So if you understand that, influencing is helping others do right.

Doing the right things are basic expectations. As an individual I come to work on time, I have a good attitude, I'm reliable, I do good quality, I'm efficient. Those are all basic expectations, do things right, and that's really what you have to do to be successful. And the next thing is do the right things. So I can be valuable, but I could not work. So as I talk about contribution and doing the right things, it's about judgement, a broader view, and moving towards influencing, which is helping others do the right things. Being a day-maker, help others' day be better, and drive the results that we need. Encourage others to assume innocence and learn more skills and be a better contributor versus just myself. And that's really the highest level of contribution. It's not just myself I'm influencing, it's other.

So as we move from system to system, it's important to know that it's complicated. It takes a lot of time and effort. A lot of meetings and discussions and not just with leadership but with teams. So what do you think about this? What if we do this? What if we made this adjustment? How would that make you feel? What are your thoughts about that? So lots of agonizing discussion and thought about how to implement the right thing. Because if it's not right, it'll cause a lot of damage.

It's also important to note that it evolves. It's not like all of a sudden we came to it in one day and you roll it out. You roll it out and maybe you make tweaks. Maybe you roll out a part of it so you can in turn make adjustments without making a negative impact on the culture. As we made this evolution and we met with team members and had discussions about the system, we've trained them so we went the same evolution we're discussing today with you we've been through with team members. We've walked through the evolution and had the discussion. And had the discussion about internally fair, externally competitive. And the marketplace, just like balancing your own checkbook.

We believe that if team members have the same information that I have, they'll make the same decision that I made. So we share with that, we share with them, we show them the data and review it and have discussions openly to help drive the right results for the company as a group.

Gary Peterson

We had a need that needed to be solved and that was getting people involved in driving improvements. And so we asked ourselves, "what system will help us do that?" in this case we turned first at compensation, and it worked for us. It was a gamble, but if we can't get them bought in we can't accomplish what we want to do.

So doing that achieved our end of saying a high performer is desired at this company. And those who were high performers felt recognized for it. It also had the effect of new employees who were coming in were rising faster if they were high contributors.

So they had a reason to stay, beyond the fact that they loved the company. They loved the work, they loved the fact that they owned the work. They're rising fast in the compensation ranks and they know how they're doing. They're contributing.

As with any system, you've always got to be asking yourself, "is this still meeting our needs? Is this still doing what we want it to do?" And there are some systems that need to be retired. There are new systems that need to be created. And for now, I can't foresee any change in the future coming to our compensation system, but it will when we need it to.

This video was filled with interesting lessons learned, and once again, I hope you took copious notes. Let us compare notes with the lessons that we felt were important for us to learn.

- Systems need to change over time, depending on the purpose and objectives of the organization.
- Identifying the correct system may take numerous iterations and will not happen with your first effort.
- Extrinsic rewards can kick-start change but should gradually shift to intrinsic rewards.
- Test and tweak systems continuously as needed. It is rarely right the first time.
- System design should be influenced by meeting with and listening to the people affected.
- Training is key to help people understand why and not just the how behind changes.

But understanding the key messages of this interview is not enough. Every time we go through a video and understand the messages of the video, we should follow that by asking ourselves questions like:

- What two or three things did the video highlight which are important to you?
- What are some specific things you can take back with you when you get back to work?
- What will you do differently?

> Everything should be made as simple as possible, but not simpler.
>
> **Albert Einstein**

THREE TYPES OF SYSTEMS/SYSTEMS MAPS

The world is filled with systems. As you can see from Figure 5.6, there are environmental/ecological systems, and there are human systems. There are systems all around us, including governmental systems, driving systems, and household systems. There are systems for doing the dishes and watering the lawn. However, for the purpose of expanding our understanding of the

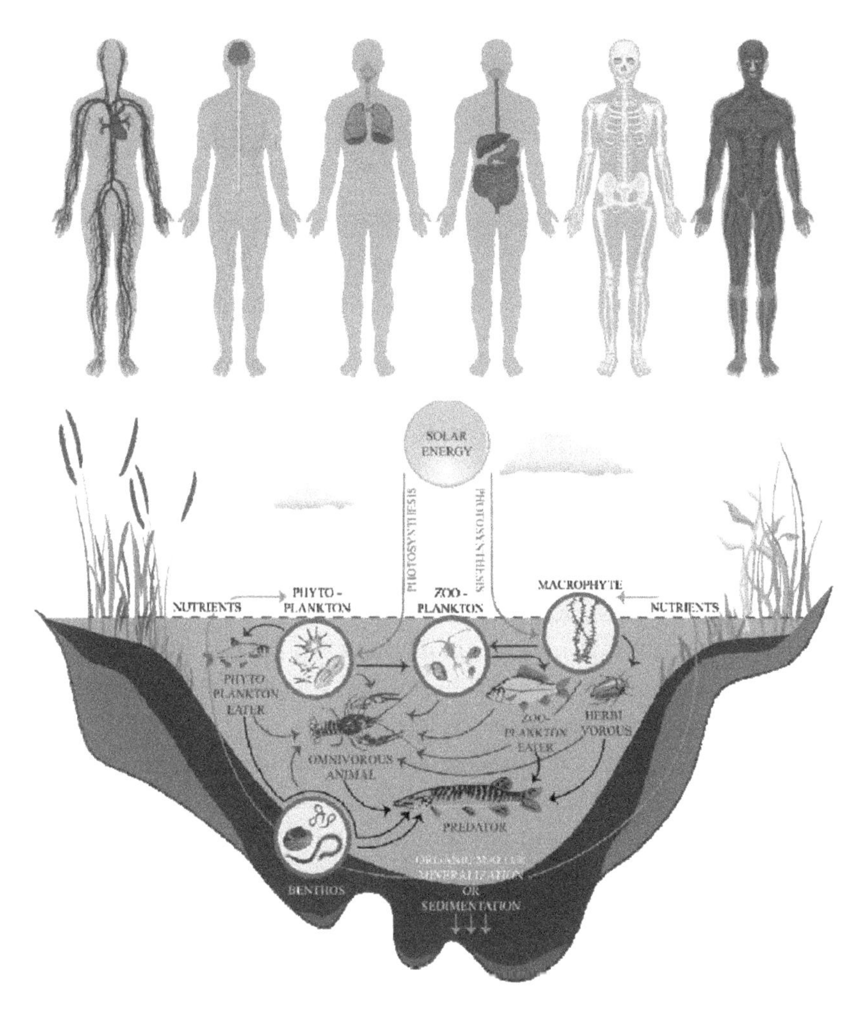

FIGURE 5.6
Systems.

Shingo methodology, we will focus on three essential types of systems that should exist in every enterprise. They are (Figure 5.7):

- Management systems – The focus is on developing leaders
- Work systems – The focus is on managing and executing workflows
- Improvement systems – The focus is on continuous improvement

The most common systems in an organization are the work systems. That is where the work happens within the organization. The second most common

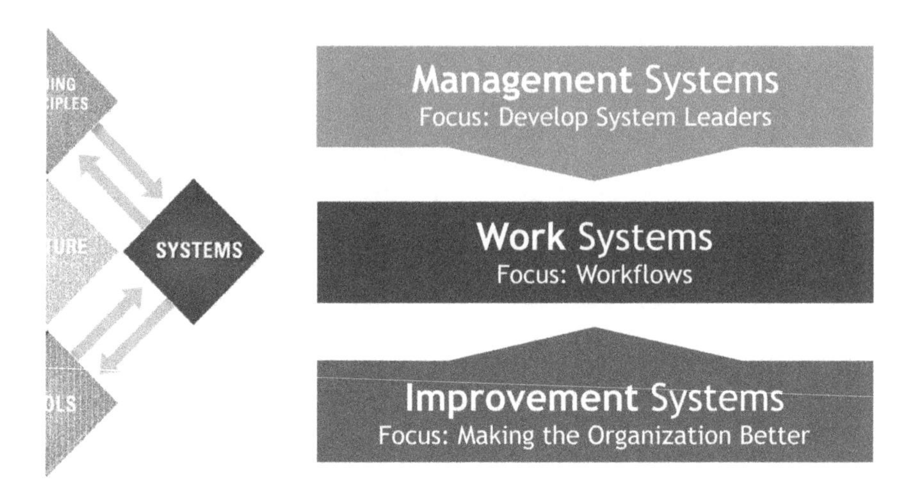

FIGURE 5.7
Three Essential Systems.

systems are the improvement systems that focus on making the organization better by driving improvement across all the work and management systems. The least common is the management system which focuses on developing leaders and provides direction to the leaders of the other systems.

Each system is dependent on the other systems. Each of the systems is highly interconnected. The Shingo Institute understands that there are many more systems that can be identified and discussed, but these three are the primary focus because they cover the most possibilities. Others would simply follow the same pattern and model.

The three types of systems are connected and interdependent on each other. Ideally, the improvement system would go across all systems within the organization as we see in Figure 5.8. Management systems develop people within the work systems they guide and the improvement subsystems they are responsible for. Work systems utilize the improvement system by focusing on improving the workflow.

As you can see, there can be multiple levels of management systems. Management systems may incorporate work systems that are the responsibility of the management system leader, for example, business development.

All systems should include five required elements. These include:

- Standard work
- Reports

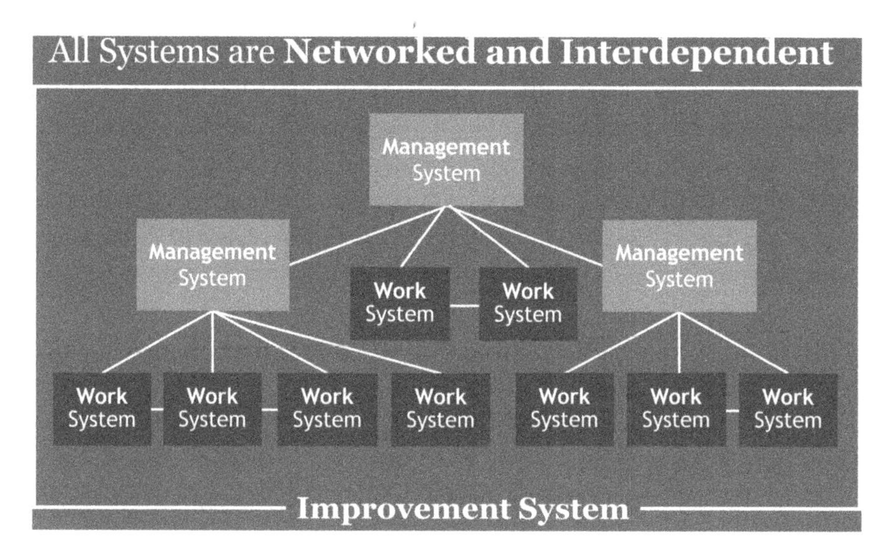

FIGURE 5.8
The System's Network.

- Feedback
- Schedule
- Improvement log

Standard work means that you have a documented sequence of the current way to do a process and that everyone does it the same way. Examples of standard work can consist of detailed work instructions, standard operating procedures, visual processes, or even checklists, etc. Standard work is used to train workers and to provide a means to audit benchmarked execution of the process. It provides a baseline for improvement.

Standard work is a basic requirement because if the way work is performed is not standardized, then it cannot be improved. If everyone does the same job function differently, then creating a new way of doing that job simply adds to the confusion and improves nothing.

Reports contain the information that is needed for the day-to-day operation of the business. Reports include information or data used in and by a system. Reports should be aligned with organizational goals and objectives. They are necessary, should be accurate, and should be visually easy to understand by everyone in the enterprise.

Feedback can be personal or for a larger group. It can be verbal or in the form of a written review.

The schedule is the timing and sequencing tool that controls the execution of the other tools. A schedule is a cadence of repetitive actions, such as meetings and reviews. For example, if you do not schedule improvement, it does not happen. Each system has a cadence or schedule of its own. This cadence (rhythm, tempo, meter, measure, rise and fall, beat, pulse, rhythmical flow, or rhythmical pattern) includes the frequency of review of the standard work, of reports, of the feedback mechanism, of the improvement log, and of the measurements. Schedule discipline is key to improving any system.

The key to successful improvements is to have an improvement log that captures improvement ideas as they come up. An improvement log is a document that captures improvement opportunities. In far too many cases, people express great ideas, but these ideas vanish because no one captures them. Listing an idea on an improvement is authorization to do research on that idea. It is not the approval of an idea. A formal proposal will need to be presented and approved before additional resources are assigned (Figure 5.9).

Figure 5.10 gives us an example of a Work System Map. System maps are examples of how an organization can structure system components

FIGURE 5.9
Basic Systems Requirements.

Work System Map	
Work System	**Work System Leader**
Shipping	Amy
Aim	
Ship finished goods safely, on-time, and without errors or damage. Engage everyone in continuous improvement.	
Workflows	
Full truckload, less than truckload, parcel, export	
Team Members	
Shippers, receivers, loaders, dispatch, inventory specialists	

Schedule															
Feedback	Frequency	9/30	9/30	10/7	10/14	10/21	10/28	11/4	11/11	11/18	11/25	12/2	12/9	12/16	12/23
Shift Huddle	Daily	D	D	D	D	D	D	D	D	D	D	D	D	D	D
Leads Review	Daily	D	D	D	D	D	D	D	D	D	D	D	D	D	D
Staff Meeting	Weekly	X	X	X	X	X	X	X	X	X	X	X	X	X	X
Go & Observe Walk	Bi-Weekly			X		X		X		X			X		X
Review Imp. Log	Bi-Weekly	X	X		X		X		X			X		X	
Review Measurements	Monthly			X				X				X			
Review WS Map	Quarterly							X							

Standard Work	Reports	Imp. Sub-Systems	Work System Improvement Log	Assign	Due
Truck Load Work Inst.	Shift Report	Idea Generation	5S project for Building H-1	George	10/28
LTL Work Inst.	Quality Report	Training	Audit work instructions for on-line shipments	Susan	11/11
Parcel Work Inst.	Accident Reports	5S	Create training materials for new shipping hires	Frank	10/14
International Work Inst.	Forms	Visual Management	Research shipping damage on export orders	Juan	10/14
Online Shipments	Orders	Problem Solving			
	Database Queries	Voice of the Customer			
	Display Boards	Safety			

Key Performance Indicators	Goal	July	Aug	Sept	Oct	Nov	Dec	Key Behavioral Indicators
Ship on-time	95%	94%	96%	90%				Exceptions to on-time delivery are noted and PDCA performed
Quality correct shipments to customer	99%	97%	98%	96%				Standard work for account routing is followed
Quality ship without product damage	99%	96%	94%	95%				Standard work for shipping is followed and validated
Safety hours between accidents	10K	9.7K	15K	20K				Near misses are reported and resolved
Idea Generation (1 per month per employee)	42	40	55	38				Ideas are documented as they occur

FIGURE 5.10
Work System Map Example.

and tools. This is the example that the Shingo Institute uses, but there are other ways to do this, e.g., in a Word document or a spreadsheet formatted differently. This example shows the structure necessary for understanding a work system. Similar maps can be made for other types of systems. To fully understand how the system map works would take a book by itself. The best way to understand system maps is by attending the Shingo Systems course, where you go out on the production floor and analyze a system using this mapping process and thereby get a complete understanding of the systems analysis process.

Let me highlight just a few important elements of the Work System Map in Figure 5.10. The Actual Work Systems Map that you will receive in the System Workshop (https://shingo.org/education/systems-design) are in color. These documents that you will receive from the Shingo Institute will be color coded. Headings in the map are color coded to match the Shingo Model (https://shingo.org/shingo-model) diamonds. In this model, Guiding Principles are blue, Systems are in green, Tools are red, Results are gold, and Culture is in purple. Since we are working with a work system, the upper left-hand corner system definition box is in green. Here we see the name of the work system, the work system leader, the goal or aim of the system, its workflows, and its team members.

Continuing our discussion of the colors, moving down we see in red the standard work and the reports that come out of the system. In green, we see the improvement subsystems that audit the improvement process relevant for this system. In the upper right in red we see the feedback mechanisms and the schedules relevant for this system. Below that, also in red, we have the Work Systems Improvement Log, along with the assignee and the due date. Across the bottom we have the KPIs showing how this system has been performing. We also have some KBIs listed which are what the employees get measured on and how they are motivated in response to the system's performance. These, of course, need to be validated against the goals of the enterprise. You can see from this review of the systems map that all the five required elements are reported as a system's review is performed using this tool.

Organizations need to adapt the systems map so it works best for them. Formalizing the system is what is most important, and this is done by documenting the components and tools in whatever format they choose.

A Harvard Business Review article, dated September/October 1999, titled *Decoding the DNA of the Toyota Production System* and written by Steven Spear and H. Kent Bowen listed the following TPS rules:

- Rule 1: All work is highly specified in its content, sequence, timing, and outcome.
- Rule 2: Each worker knows who provides what and when.
- Rule 3: Every product and service flows along a simple, specified path.
- Rule 4: Any improvement to process, worker/machine connections, or flow path must be made through the scientific method, under a teacher's guidance, and in the lowest possible organizational level.

These rules seem simple and basic, but they are often ignored. However, they are critical in the performance of an effective and high performing system.

Let me conclude with a story that I experienced during an overseas assignment with the largest company in the world. The project was focused on reducing bureaucracy, and one example of a systems failure occurred in their purchase order approval process. When a purchase order was created, it needed 16 signatures in order for the purchase order to move forward and the approval process would take six to eight months. The question that everyone needed to ask immediately was where did the 16 come from and the answer is "tradition." Informal tradition within the company caused every process failure to be corrected by adding another checkpoint. So, whenever there was a failure in the purchase order process, the traditional solution was to add another signature to the purchase order procedure in the hope that this additional signature would prevent the failure in the future. Another checkpoint was added. These additional checkpoints caused the process to take longer, and the result was 16 signatures over a six-to-eight-month period.

In the team's effort to reduce the bureaucracy of this process, possibly by automation, they decided to interview each of the 16 individuals and ask them what that individual looked at to see if the purchase order should be approved, and each one of the sixteen individuals said something to the effect that they just checked to see if a certain other individual had approved the purchase order, then they were sure it would be correct. The net effect was that no one actually looked at the purchase order, and its approval went through as if no one would have signed anything. But it took six to eight months to accomplish this failure.

Here we have a system, driven by traditional corrective action procedures, that had created an enormous bureaucracy and had still failed to achieve the goals and objectives of the organization. The entire system was a waste. It was replaced by one auditor who had a checklist of things to check on the purchase order, and then he would give approval for the purchase order to move forward. A six-to-eight-month process had been reduced to two weeks.

This example seems obscenely stupid; however, it took an outsider to see how stupid it really was. And before you laugh too loudly, you may want to look at a couple of the processes within your own enterprise where the solution to failure was to incorporate another checkpoint, thereby adding additional complication to the process, causing the process to take longer, and adding an additional point where failure could occur.

> A bad system will beat a good person every time.
>
> We are being ruined by the best efforts of people who are doing the wrong thing.
>
> It is not enough to do your best; you must know what to do, and then do your best.
>
> Best efforts will not substitute for knowledge.
>
> **W. Edwards Deming**

DEFINITION OF A GOOD SYSTEM

At this point, it is a valuable exercise for the reader to reflect back on the previous discussions of a system and make a list of what constitutes a "Good System." Everyone would end up with their own unique list. A starting point might be the list that the author promotes, which is:

1. It creates value for the customer.
2. It aligns with the purpose and organizational objectives.
3. It is informed by principles.
4. It drives good behaviors.
5. It integrates and reinforces other systems (Ackoff).

6. It evolves over time (Peterson).
7. Always make the right thing easier to do than the wrong thing.
8. It is documented and repeatable through standard work.
9. It is the best-known way of doing something.
10. It has an owner who is accountable.
11. It is as simple as possible.
12. It is understood by workers.
13. It motivates.
    a. Measurement System
14. It has performance standards, and results are measured and reported.
15. Employees receive feedback and recognition from the system.
16. A constant search for Continuous Improvement.
    a. Waste Elimination
17. Management/leadership understands the system.

Shingo Principles are applied through the systems that you design and implement. Building systems based on the Shingo Guiding Principles gives us a proven roadmap for success. Some of the lessons this chapter has taught us about building systems include:

- Building systems that drive behavior is a "Team Effort."
- There are often multiple systems that focus on the behavior that we are trying to modify. Systems are not mutually exclusive.
- The selection of an ideal system focused on the ideal behavior is an iterative process.
- A good system validates the correlation of the KBIs to the ideal behavior.
- The role of managers is to spend their time focused on identifying the correct KBIs (more on this in the next chapter).
- Motivating correct behavior through systems changes continues to close the gap between current behavior and ideal behavior, which in turn shifts the culture.

SUMMARY

This chapter is filled with lessons learned, and there are numerous key points highlighted throughout the chapter. I will relist some here as a summary, but for the supporting details you will need to go back through the respective chapter discussions.

From Russell L. Ackoff we learned:

- The failure to meet customer expectations results from anti-systemic thinking.
- A system is a whole – the sum of its parts.
- The parts of a system are interdependent and interconnected and cannot be divided into its parts and still function.
- The essential or defining properties of any system are properties of the whole which none of its parts have.
- An improvement system that is directed at improving the parts taken separately may improve the performance of that part, but the performance of the whole will not be improved.
- An improvement program must be directed at what you want, not at what you don't want. Determining what you want requires you to redesign the system. Fixing a system defect will not fix the overall system.

From Gary Peterson and David Siebert we learned:

- Systems need to change over time, depending on the purpose and objectives of the organization.
- Extrinsic rewards can kick-start change but should gradually shift to intrinsic rewards.
- Test and tweak systems as needed. It's usually not right the first time.
- System design should be influenced by meeting with and listening to the people affected.
- Training is key to help people understand changes.

At this point, the reader should start to see the interconnectedness between the various elements of the Shingo methodology. As you move through this book, you will continue to see that the Shingo Model is not a series of isolated boxes or tools, but it is an integrated methodology which ties all these five boxes together to create the bridge to success. No piece is redundant or unnecessary. Each has a vital role. But each cannot stand alone. The pieces need each other in order to create an integrated methodology that will drive the organization to continuously improve Enterprise Excellence.

> It's the easiest thing in the world to argue logically that something is impossible. It is much more difficult to ask how something might be accomplished, to transcend its difficulties, and to imagine how it might be made possible. Go all out in pursuit of ways to do the impossible.
>
> **Shigeo Shingo**

6

Metrics

The most stupendous improvement plans in the world will be ineffective unless they are translated into practice. Often at this stage the resistance of habit will prevent shop workers from implementing improvement plans. Indeed, such plans cannot be fully realized unless consent is obtained along with understanding and unless tenacious efforts are sustained.

Shigeo Shingo

ANOTHER REFLECTION

Another example of shifting cultures and shifting behaviors was found in a hospital project that the author was involved with. In this case, the hospital president and his senior staff were directed by their board to come up with a strategic plan. The board was frustrated by the long wait times and high costs of the hospital's operation, and they wanted to get it under control. Potential patients preferred to go to nearby hospitals which were more responsive to patient's needs. The hospital leadership was directed to put a focus on improving customer quality, which included responsiveness, and cost reduction.

The author led the strategy workshops, which were a series of half-day workshops, each week over a month. A preferred off-site two-day option was deemed unacceptable by the hospital administration. However, the space between the sessions worked to the advantage of the author in that it allowed intermediate time for data collection. In the end, the weekly meetings continued well past the two months.

The hospital leadership was convinced that what they needed to do was focus on cost and run some RIEs on the inventory stockrooms, and that this would identify where the cost waste was occurring. The author was not in agreement. He challenged them to focus first on customer satisfaction and identify where customer failures were occurring, and that costs would be reduced by first focusing on the hospital's culture and their attitude about customer satisfaction. Hospital administration was slightly offended at the idea that maybe they were not as responsive to their patient's needs as they should have been. The author stressed that their looking at cost as a higher priority than customer satisfaction exemplified that the culture was pointed in the wrong direction.

The author challenged the leadership to start by focusing on customer satisfaction, starting by looking first at their highest priced real estate. This, of course, was the OR (Operating Room). They were currently using a scheduling methodology for OR where doctors blocked off a segment of time, and that time was locked up for that doctor, no matter how little of that time he or she actually utilized. In conjunction with the leadership of the hospital, a new scheduling system was designed that would allow smaller time segments whose length was specific to the procedure that would be performed. Using a Gemba approach of "Go and Observe," they also realized that a lot of what was done in the OR (preparation and cleanup work) could be done outside of the OR either before or after the procedure. By making these basic changes, and after about three months of using the new scheduling methodology, the hospital was able to triple the amount of procedures that were being run through the OR, significantly reducing the cost of each procedure and enormously increasing utilization and capacity. And, of course, customer satisfaction was improved when patients no longer needed to wait months for the care they needed.

Then the strategy team moved on to the next most expensive real estate in the hospital, which was the ER (Emergency Room). Similar Gemba observations of the ER quickly identified that the delays in the ER were caused primarily due to a lack of responsiveness of the labs and a lack of efficiency in scheduling beds in the main hospital. Patients would be on hold in the ER for hours, waiting for lab work or waiting for a bed. And this made turnaround in the ER extremely slow. The Gemba, Go and Observe, shifted to a focus on studying the lab systems and the bed scheduling systems. In the end, the poor performance of both of these systems turned out to be the result of the labs and bed schedulers, not knowing the impact that they were having on ER. They had not been able to see the big picture. No one was watching the performance of the overall ER flow and the systems connected with that flow. The lab changed several of their procedures, focusing on improving their responsiveness to ER, and bed scheduling also changed procedures which allowed the ER improved information on bed availability. Once again, now that the big system perspective had been identified and appropriate changes were made to the various subsystems, performance was dramatically affected. Wait time in the ER waiting room was reduced from, in the worst case, several hours down to minutes. The ER soon prided itself on trying to keep wait times down to single digit minutes.

The big change that occurred was in the culture. Hospital leadership no longer focused on cost reduction, previously thinking of themselves as a factory. They realized that customer satisfaction needed to be the focus. Along with this, the cultural transformation of the leadership trickled down to management and the associates. Each felt more pride in their work when their customers were satisfied with the reduced response times and the improved results.

The other big change was the systems perspective, where the hospital saw itself as a large patient response system, with numerous interconnecting subsystems, each of which affected the overall performance of the larger system. This new systems perspective changed the way hospital leadership thought of their specific roles. The hospital was no longer focused on keeping doctors happy. Administration and the doctors all shifted their focus to keeping the patient's happy, and that turned out be a major critical cultural shift.

The author stepped out of this project at this point, which was about six months into the transformation effort, but leadership continued having their weekly strategy meetings and made that a permanent part of their new culture. They continued working and reworking the different systems within the hospital.

THE BUILDING BLOCKS OF CULTURAL SHIFT

At this point, we have learned a lot about the connection between purpose, principles, systems, and behaviors. If we reflect back on Figure 5.1, where we have the Three Shingo Insights listed, we learned that:

1. Ideal Results Require Ideal Behavior

2. Purpose and Systems Drive Behavior
3. Principles Inform Ideal Behavior

Building on these insights and the learnings from previous chapters, we can expand on them and flip them allowing us to state the following (Figure 6.1):

1. Principles inform behaviors and are, therefore, manifest in behaviors.
2. Purpose and systems drive behaviors.
3. We need to create systems that drive behaviors ever closer to ideal.

From these learnings, we are driven to the conclusion:

> Behaviors need to align to the Purpose, the Guiding Principles, and to the Goals of the organization.

As we continue our discussion of driving toward a Shingo Enterprise Excellent environment, we next focus on metrics. However, we cannot forget that metrics are a part of a system. They are not independent. The system incorporates metrics as the motivators, keeping whatever happens within the system aligned with the goals. Hence, as we continue our

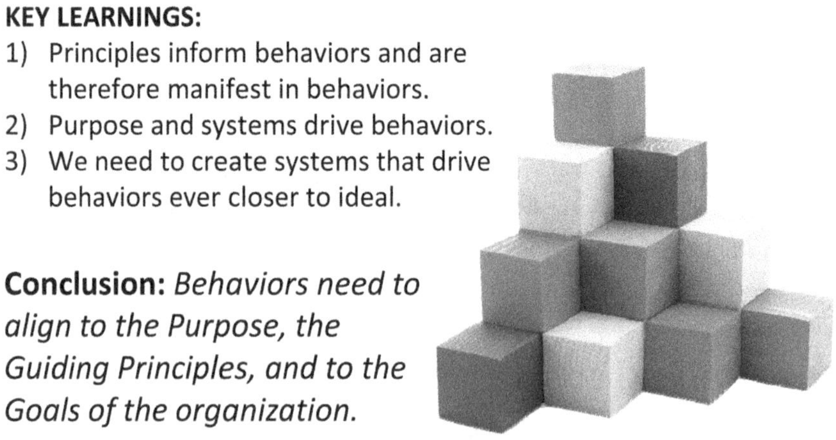

KEY LEARNINGS:
1) Principles inform behaviors and are therefore manifest in behaviors.
2) Purpose and systems drive behaviors.
3) We need to create systems that drive behaviors ever closer to ideal.

Conclusion: *Behaviors need to align to the Purpose, the Guiding Principles, and to the Goals of the organization.*

FIGURE 6.1
The Building Blocks of Culture Shift.

discussion, we will repeatedly see how systems are actively involved in whatever metrics we create.

Behaviors are modified and adjusted by systems. A leader's role is to make sure that the systems are driving behaviors closer to the ideal behavior. This is an excellent time to reflect back on Figure 4.3, redrawn here as Figure 6.2, in order to make sure we understand the linkage between KBIs (key behavioral indicators) and KPIs (key performance indicators). The pillar which supports a sustainable culture is built on a foundation of principles which generates KBI results. Both pillars, one based on tools and one based on principles, are necessary for us to be able to migrate across the bridge toward success. Identifying the correct ideal behaviors, and then designing systems to drive those ideal behaviors, is a key learning objective of this chapter. The behaviors that leaders are trying to drive through the systems should be measurable as KBIs. Appropriately selected and defined behaviors should then drive results which should be measurable as KPIs.

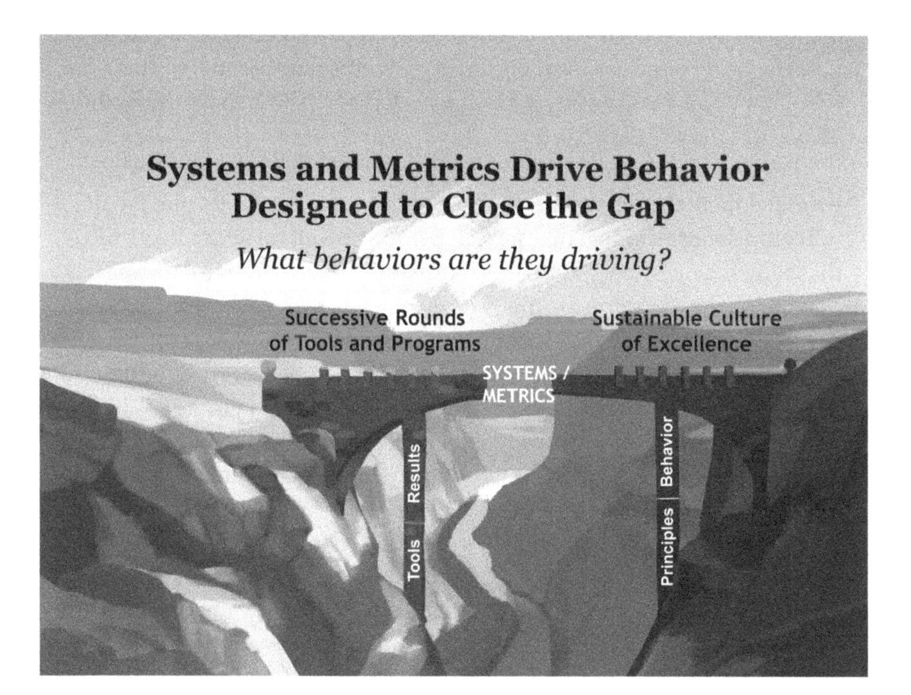

FIGURE 6.2
The Shingo Bridge to Success.

Now that we have a clearer understanding of the connection between KPIs and KBIs, let us return to our discussion of the building blocks of a cultural shift. We now understand how systems drive behavior. As a brief supporting reminder, the Discover Excellence workshop contains a video which gives examples of how systems drive behavior. We will repeat the text of that video here primarily because, at this point, in the learning process, we are convinced that this video will take on an entirely new level of significance for you, the reader.

Presented by **Gerhard Plenert, Previous Director of Executive Education**, The Shingo Institute

We talk about how systems drive behavior and how important it is to align systems to principles. Have you ever noticed in your personal life or work environment how a policy, or a system focused around a policy, keeps growing?

It keeps getting bigger, more complex, and more difficult to administer. We've experienced that numerous times.

One example of systems failure occurred at a factory that had horrible quality problems. Their reject rate was enormous and the CEO asked us to visit the facility and review their quality systems in order to find the solutions. They had quality posters and quotes hanging throughout the facility. They had a quality department.

After taking a tour and listening about how quality conscious they were, we asked them the telling question, "How are your employees measured?"

Their response was that they were measured on units produced. So I asked the follow-up question, "Who fixes the quality issues?" And the answer was that the quality department analyzed the failures at the end of the production process and fixed the problems. In this system, the line workers were not responsible for or rewarded for quality. They were rewarded for pumping out units. All that mattered to them was the number of units produced, regardless of whether they were good or bad.

The reward system in this facility drove the undesirable behavior of ignoring quality. Failures were never connected to the source of the problem. The employee reward and measurement system was then changed to measure the quality of the units produced and magically the defect rate shrunk dramatically. Suddenly, employees became more conscious of the quality they produced because it directly affected their paycheck.

Another example of poor systems causing poor results occurred in the purchasing office of one of the world's largest oil and gas conglomerates. In this case, because of a history of inaccurate purchase orders, a series of controls were put in place to make sure that all purchase orders were properly vetted. A purchase order now required 16 approval signatures before it could be released.

The process of routing this document often took six to eight months. Our role as consultants to this organization was to streamline the process, and we started by asking each of the 16 signees what they looked for on the document in order to determine whether or not to sign it. We were surprised when every one of the 16 told us that all they looked for was that another specific individual had signed the document. If so, they were sure the purchase order had to be correct.

In the end, they had 16 control points for every purchase order, all of which created waste, time delay, and none of which added value, since none of them actually checked the document. The failed system drove this behavior because it caused a false sense of security for all the signees.

Were either of these examples following the Shingo Guiding Principles of creating value for the customer or assured quality at the source? Of course not. It would've been better if only one trusted purchase order signee, who knew they were responsible for the accuracy of the document, reviewed the document carefully rather than having 16 signees who didn't care.

This reminds us of a Lean philosophy that states, "Always make the right thing easier to do than the wrong thing." A system that is too complex can easily be defeated. It is important to recognize the connections between principles, systems, and behavior. Systems drive behavior. And even with the correct principles, if we don't have the proper supporting systems, we won't get the desired ideal behaviors.

So far in this and the previous chapter, we have cited numerous examples of how systems and metrics drive behaviors. Failures are rarely the fault of individuals. Failures occur because individuals are trying to work with, and often trying to work around, an incompetent system. What is the next step in creating a successful systems operating environment? Normal reactions are to "Fix the System." Fixing the system usually means that we insert another step into the system which is often some type of control point, thereby adding to the complexity of the system, increasing the total processing lead time, and introducing another potential failure point. However, the correct solution for fixing a failing system is found in a much higher approach. That higher approach asks the question, "What should ideal behavior look like?" This approach challenges us with questions like, "Should we scrap this system completely?", which often occurs when we have an overabundance of control points as in the purchase order example near the end of the last chapter. Or, "Should we completely redesign the system starting at ground zero?"

When creating or fixing a system and its metrics, we need to start the change process by focusing on two questions:

1. What does "ideal behavior" look like?
2. How do we move closer to this ideal behavior by redesigning systems and their corresponding metrics?

Motivating correct behavior by redesigning systems continues to close the gap between current behavior and ideal behavior, which in turn shifts the culture. Systems are multidimensional. A positive effect in one area may generate a negative effect somewhere else, as we saw in Figure 5.4. In any systems redesign, we need to move to as high a level as possible, making sure the entire network of systems is improved. Remembering some of the key messages that came out of the Russell L. Ackoff video from Chapter 5 were that:

- A system is a whole – the sum of its parts.
- The parts of a system are interdependent and interconnected and cannot be divided into its parts and still function.
- The essential or defining properties of any system are properties of the whole which none of its parts have.
- An improvement system that is directed at improving the parts taken separately may improve the performance of that part, but the performance of the whole will not be improved.

KBIs AND KPIs

As has already been discussed several times, KBIs (key behavioral indicators) are used to measure adjustments in the transformation of behaviors (Figure 6.3). These adjustments are triggered by systems modifications. But ultimately, the KPIs are the external world's measure of enterprise performance. We need to build KBIs which will not only focus on desired behaviors but will also ultimately achieve the KPI success that we need as an enterprise. This balance of metrics is often very difficult to

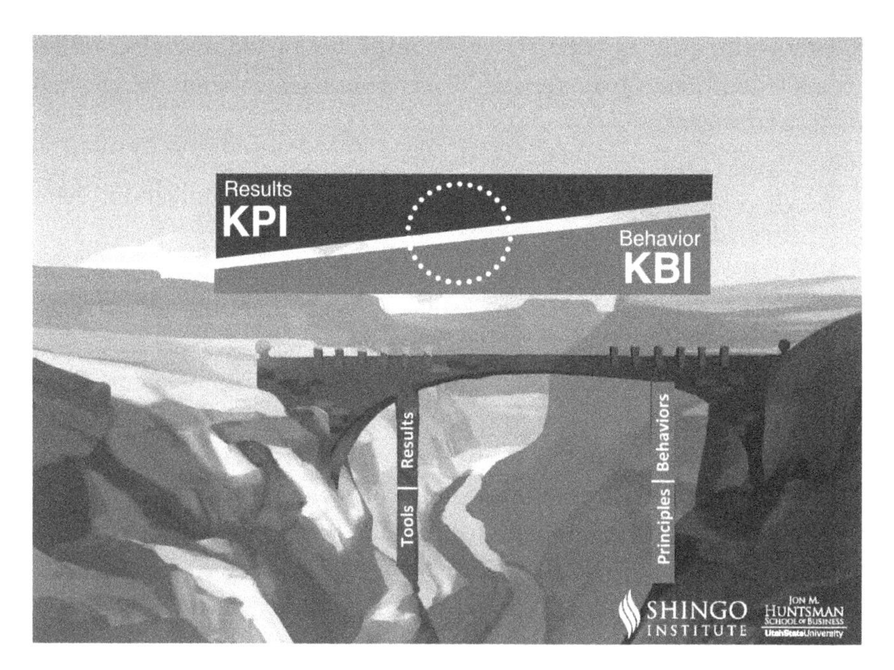

FIGURE 6.3
The Link between KBIs and KPIs.

achieve and may require several iterations before a successful combination can be found.

Saying all of this in a slightly different way, KBIs are leading indicators, whereas KPIs are lagging indicators. KPIs are lagging because they tell us about how we performed in the past. KBIs are leading because they help us adjust and transform the future. This chapter discusses the linkages between the two.

WHAT MAKES A GOOD ASSESSMENT?

We begin our discussion of KPIs and KBIs by recognizing that both KPIs and KBIs are assessments of our ongoing (in the case of KBIs) and past (in the case of KPIs) performance. We next need to ask ourselves the question, "What metrics constitute a good assessment of our performance?" You should stop reading here and make your own list. Then come back to the chapter and see our suggested answers to this question.

After listing your answers to what constitutes a good assessment, here are a few additional characteristics of a good assessment tool that you may want to consider:

- The assessment must provide value to the organization being assessed.
- It must offer a good analysis of results so that the organization can understand what level they are at and where they are not currently performing.
- The assessment must assess behaviors (KBIs); it cannot be just about results (KPIs). It needs to give feedback about how the results are being achieved. Are the improvements sustainable?
- Is there a purpose manifested in the behaviors observed?
- Are the supporting systems driving ideal behaviors? Are they making it easier to do the right thing than the wrong thing?
- What are the gaps in both results and behaviors?
- It would be helpful if the assessment assisted the organization in knowing who owns the gaps? Who is responsible? How will they close the gap? How do you set priorities?

KBIs AND KPIs REVISITED

The following summarizes what we have learned so far in an attempt to draw everything together. It is important that the reader understands these connections and linkages. You cannot move forward until you understand how everything you have learned up to this point fits together. Let us review each of these points:

1. Principles inform ideal behaviors – Principles tell us what ideal behaviors should look like. In the workshops, we spend a lot of time discussing how the ten Shingo Principles should manifest themselves.
2. Systems, enabled by tools, drive behaviors (KBIs) and behaviors (KBIs) drive results (KPIs) – Earlier in this book, we spent an extensive amount of time discussing how systems utilize tools to drive behaviors. If you are still struggling with this concept,

please revert back to the previous chapters. Additionally, we have had several discussions about how KPIs are the backward-looking performance measures that stakeholders external to our company utilize in order to review performance. We also know that KBIs influence the behaviors that eventually influence KPIs. And, since KBIs are forward looking, we can use them to take corrective action before it is too late and our KPIs condemn us.

3. KBIs are *leading* indicators – A leading indicator is one that allows us to look ahead. In a sense it helps us predict the future. One of our favorite simplistic examples of leading versus lagging indicators can be a forecast of how many toilets to build. We can look at a lagging indicator, like how many toilets we built last year, and use that to predict how many toilets to build. Or you can look at a leading indicator, like the number of housing permits that have been given out and use that to predict the number of toilets to build.
4. KPIs are *lagging* indicators – As already discussed, KPIs are the metrics that the stakeholders of a company utilize to evaluate the enterprises' performance. They are what the outside world looks at when they are assessing us. They look to the past, like sales, profits, ROI (Return on Investment), and ROE (Return on Equity). But they have limited usefulness in helping an organization take corrective action early enough to make a difference.
5. Both KBIs and KPIs are measurable – In order to be of value as an assessment tool and in order to be able to take corrective action, both KBIs and KPIs need to be measurable and monitorable.

MOVING THE NEEDLE

The Build Excellence workshop, the last in the Shingo series of workshops, contains a video which shows a step-by-step progression of how starting with principles can lead to the right systems, tools, behaviors, and then to results. Here is the transcript of that video (reprinted with Gary Peterson's permission):

Gary Peterson, Executive Vice President (See Figure 6.4)

FIGURE 6.4
OC Tanner's Gary Peterson.

Supply Chain & Production
OC Tanner Headquarters

With the strategy deployment the idea now is that the teams know what to work on and they're saying that they are going to accomplish certain outcomes all that rolls up into the metrics that we are going to measure for the period and that's what we have here in our lagging metrics; the things that we think will come out of it. But we found that when we used to focus just on these final outcomes we really couldn't figure out exactly what the connection was to them, and that's when we realized that we have to really needed to focus on a leading metric, so for every lagging measurement we've identified what is the lead metric that we think if we do that this result will come. So for example right here is our safety we're looking at total injuries and OSHA recordables. I want those to fall and they have been falling for years. The question is, "How do I impact that?" and we're thinking that the way to do it is by focusing on safety catches from all of our team members, thinking that the more things they catch the more these injuries will go down. So the whole emphasis is not here, the whole emphasis is on increasing the number of safety catches. I don't think safety catches will work. Now this is all guess work. A lead metric usually is trying to guess what you think, what is the lever that if I push this the lag metric will get better. But I think this will drive it not just because you eliminate unsafe safety practices but because if everyone is doing safety catches they become more safety minded and because of that these lag metrics get better. The same thing with the quality. We've got the quality metrics. We are trying to impact customer returns. But where is the focus? The focus is, in our case, is on auditing the product and seeing the failures and seeing what's wrong. And trying to increase the number of audits on a regular basis we think will improve the quality. If you get to the end of the period and this hasn't done it you may have the wrong leading metric and that's okay, you pick another leading metric. Eventually you find the one (leading indicator) with a little bit of pressure here starts to move this metric (the lagging indicator) and that's the idea.

As a review, you need to consider the following questions:

1. What was Gary's central message? What are the main points?
    - Identify and focus on a leading metric that supports and moves the lagging metric.
    - Understand the difference between KBIs and KPIs.
    - Understand the difference between leading indicators and lagging indicators and how they should be utilized. As motivators? As dashboard and scorecard are tools for performance reviews? etc.
2. What two or three things did Gary highlight which are important to you?
    - Shifting your organization's focus from lagging to leading metrics is important.
    - The first leading metric you pick may not necessarily be the right one and you may have to use trial and error to eventually find the correct metric.
    - There must be a measurable connection between the leading and the lagging metrics.
3. What are some specific things you can take back and use to work?
    - Start a search for leading metrics which will replace the lagging metrics as motivators and drivers at the associate and management levels of the organizations.
4. What will you do differently?
    - Work on changing the mindset and culture of the organization so they can see the value of using leading metrics as motivational drivers.

ASSESSING KBIs AND KPIs

At this point it is critical to put all these learnings into practice. We do that with an exercise. As best as you can work through the following exercise, it would be helpful if you could join with other Shingo students and work this exercise as a team. There is a lot to be gained in the shared learning that would occur.

The exercise proceeds as follows:

1. Identify behaviors within your organization(s) that are driving results.
   a. Assess whether or not they are ideal?
   b. Are they measurable (KBIs)?
2. Assess the current results (KPIs) within your organization?
   a. Are they strategic (i.e., aligned to a purpose, goal, and strategy)?
   b. Assess whether or not the current behaviors are driving the correct ideal results.

In this exercise, the important part of the conversation needs to be around how KBIs drive results (KPIs) and how assessments can help identify behaviors which need to be adopted and that will drive the desired results.

Use this exercise to reflect on what behaviors are driving the results in your organization and how those behaviors compare to ideal behaviors. The purpose of this exercise is to drive home the connection between KBIs and KPIs and that it is necessary to constantly be assessing both. Only then can you identify gaps and determine corrective actions.

KBIs and KPIs need to be linked so that KBIs drive the KPIs. KPIs must be focused on the strategic objectives of the organization. KBIs, since they are leading indicators, can help us take corrective action before the KPIs inform the stakeholders that it is too late. The job of a sustainable continuous improvement enterprise is to constantly monitor the performance of both the KBIs and the KPIs and to take corrective action whenever needed by adjusting the systems that are driving the behaviors (KBIs). And that paves the road to excellence.

SUMMARY

This chapter is filled with lessons learned, and there are numerous key points highlighted throughout the chapter. I will relist them here as a summary, but for the supporting details, you will need to go back through the respective chapter discussions.

From the Three Shingo Insights we learned:

1. Principles inform behaviors and are, therefore, manifest in behaviors.
2. Purpose and systems drive behaviors.
3. We need to create systems that drive behaviors ever closer to ideal.

And additional key learnings include:

- Building systems that drive behavior is a "Team Effort."
- There are often multiple systems that focus on the behavior that we are trying to modify. Systems are not mutually exclusive.
- The selection of an ideal system focused on the ideal behavior is an iterative process.
- KBIs should link to and support the enterprises' KPIs.
- A good system validates the correlation of the KBIs to the ideal behavior.
- The role of managers is to spend their time focused on identifying the correct KBIs which motive organizational movement toward Enterprise Excellence.

> Men fear thought as they fear nothing else on earth – more than death. Thought is subversive, and revolutionary, destructive and terrible; thought is merciless to privilege, established institutions, and comfortable habits; thought is anarchic and lawless, indifferent to authority, careless to the well-tried wisdom of the ages. Thought looks into the pit of hell and is not afraid ... Thought is great and swift and free, the light of the world, and the chief glory of man. But if thought is to become the possession of the many, and not the privilege of the few, we must have done with fear. It is fear that holds men back – fear that their cherished beliefs should prove delusions, fear lest the institutions by which they live should prove harmful, fear lest they themselves prove less worthy to the respect then they have supposed themselves to be.
>
> **Bertrand Russell, Philosopher**

7

Guiding Principles

Problem identification, the first step in making improvements, involves the following concepts:

Never accept the status quo.

Find problems where you think none exist.

Work is more than people in motion.

Perceiving and thinking are not the same.

Shigeo Shingo

MORE REFLECTION

A famous international truck manufacturer (I am not going to say the name, but if you're familiar with the industry, you'll know who I'm talking about) was assessing their performance using KPIs. Each plant was evaluated and ranked based on their KPI performance. The assessment process included direct costs that could be connected directly with a plant and indirect corporate costs which were allocated across all production facilities.

After reviewing the performance of all the plants, one of the plants was losing money in that their total cost of operation (direct plus indirect costs) was greater than their revenue. The corporate decision was made to close the plant down.

Closing the plant caused indirect corporate costs, which were now allocated across one fewer production facilities. Corporate costs, of course, did not decrease with the closure of one of the plants. This, of course, meant that the operating costs (direct plus indirect) of each plant were now higher. Guess what? Another one of the production facilities, which previously was barely in the black, now found itself in the red. The decision was made to close down the facility.

This process of allocating costs and closing plants continued on until eventually the manufacturer was on the verge of bankruptcy and ended up being bought out. For us on the outside, this seems ridiculously stupid. But when viewed from the inside, where the leadership could not see the forest for the trees, it all seemed very logical.

THE LADDER OF SUCCESS

The first step in creating excellence in your enterprise is to understand the bridge to success and the principles that will sustain that success. At this point, the author assumes you have that foundational understanding and can now move forward in the creation of a plan for implementation. This book will continue to focus on giving the reader the guidance to know how to achieve a sustainable implementation methodology based on the Shingo Principles.

WHY PRINCIPLES?

The first step up the ladder to sustainable Enterprise Excellence is principles. This, of course, refers to the Shingo Principles, as discussed and taught in detail in four of the Shingo workshops. Principles, in order to be sustainable and effective, need to have the following characteristics (Figure 7.1):

- They must be universal and timeless – Principles must apply everywhere and always in order to be valid.
- They must be self-evident – We cannot invent principles, but we can *discover* them through research and study.
- Govern consequences – Regardless of our understanding of the principle, we are subject to the consequences of that principle.

- **Universal and Timeless**
  Principles apply everywhere, always.

- **Evident**
  We can't invent principles, but we can *discover* them through research and study.

- **Govern Consequences**
  Regardless of our understanding of the principle, we are subject to the consequences of that principle.

FIGURE 7.1
Characteristics of Principles.

As principles are discussed in detail in the Shingo workshops, we realized that we needed to agree on the characteristics of the ten principles in the Shingo Model. We also needed to agree that a Guiding Principle is:

- A truth that guides decisions and actions. A principle is a higher truth that goes beyond our ability to believe or not believe in the principle. It carries consequences with it.
- A foundational rule that has an inevitable consequence. We agree that we can choose whether or not we will follow the principle, but we cannot control the consequence that comes with our choice.

We also realize that principles are not stand-alone and unique. They are often interrelated. The consequences of following or not following a principle often affect the behavior of other principles. Another thing that we learned in the prior workshops is that all ten principles are not of equal importance. We should never try to place the same amount of emphasis on each principle. Every organization is different, and the amount of effort we place on a principle and its timing often differ. And that is important because not all organizations are at the same point in their journey to sustainable Enterprise Excellence. A customized effort, favoring one principle at one time in the journey, and emphasizing another principle at a different time, becomes critical.

THE SHINGO MODEL – A REVIEW

In Figure 7.2, we see:

- The three insights for Enterprise Excellence
- The Shingo Model (the diamond)
- The Shingo Principles (the triangle at the top half of the Guiding Principles square) broken out into three dimensions in a triangle to the top right.

As a review, we need to walk through the details of the Shingo Model and its various components. The connectivity and interaction between each of the pieces is critical when trying to understand how the model works. Most important of all is the center of the model, the culture which is defined by and built upon the behaviors of the individuals within the enterprise. We define what we want this culture to look like by establishing a set of Guiding Principles,

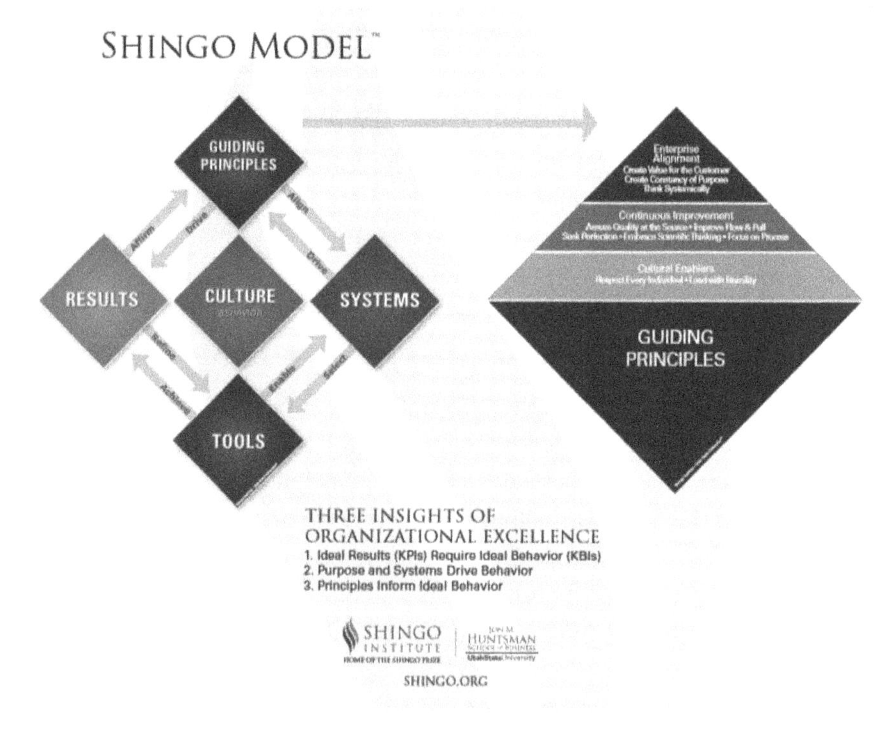

FIGURE 7.2
The Shingo Model.

which are specific to our enterprise. By carefully defining the principles, we establish what we are ultimately driving our enterprise toward.

In Figure 7.2, we see the top square highlights the principles. This is where we start when trying to understand the Shingo methodology. These Guiding Principles are foundational in defining what is important to your enterprise. The Shingo Institute has offered its recommendation for what these ten principles should look like. But every organization needs to identify its own set of principles. These ten from Shingo are simply recommendations, and each of the principles listed by Shingo should somehow become incorporated into the Guiding Principles that you develop for your enterprise.

Next, based on these Guiding Principles, the enterprise needs to define its vision, mission, and strategy, primarily using KPIs that are consistent with the expectations of stakeholders, stockholders, customers, and anyone else in the world outside of the enterprise that is observing the performance of the enterprise. With the strategy in place, drive (see the arrow pointing from Guiding Principles toward Results) is added to the Results square, which is at the left-hand corner of the model. Performance results Affirm (also an arrow) that the Guiding Principles are being supported.

Next comes one of the hardest parts of building an Enterprise Excellence model. We jump from the left side of the model which is the Results, to the right side of the model which is the Systems. As we have seen in an earlier chapter, the systems within an organization drive the behaviors of the individuals within an organization. We have also learned that these systems require motivational metrics and that these metrics need to be focused on futuristic ideal behaviors. A drive toward ideal behaviors is only possible by using KBIs. But these KBIs need to be dual purposed. They need to drive ideal behaviors, and at the same time, they need to support the KBIs that were defined earlier in the Results section of the model. As we see in the model, Systems Drive (the arrow) us toward correct Guiding Principles, and these principles need to be Aligned (another arrow) with the Systems.

The last square in the model is Tools, and that is exactly what they are. There is a plethora of TPS tools, and these are the tools that should be used to identify, define, and refine the Systems, constantly checking to make sure that the enabled Systems are able to achieve the desired Results. Depending on what system is being studied, the Continuous Improvement Specialist in your organization is expected to have an understanding of the dozens of tool options and is expected to be able to select the best set of tools for the analysis of the particular system under consideration.

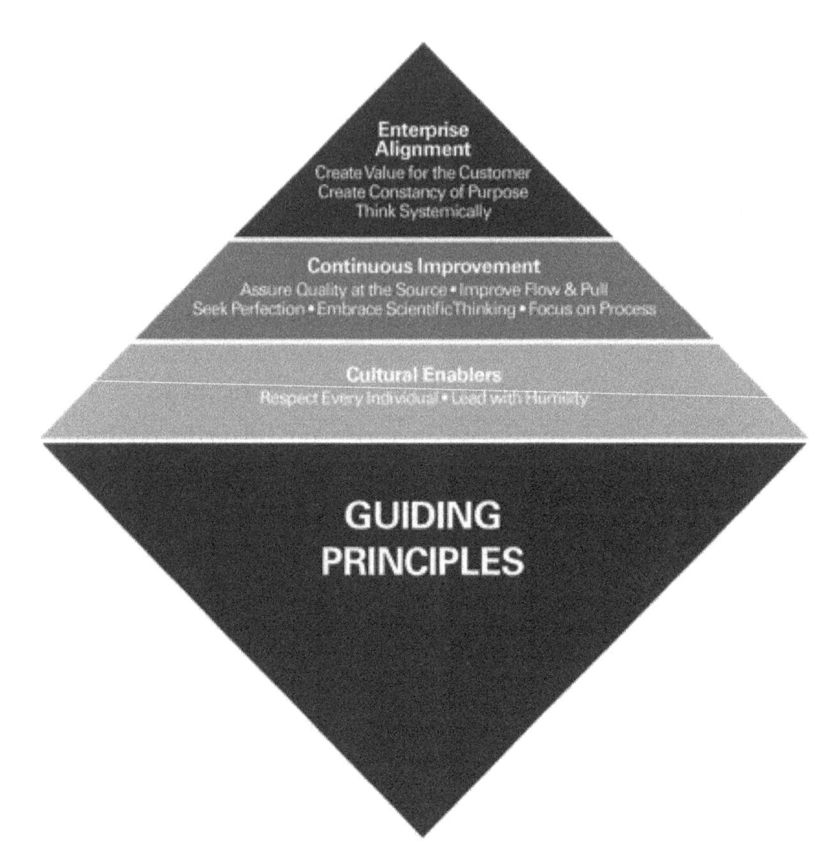

FIGURE 7.3
The Shingo Model Guiding Principles.

Having reviewed the Shingo Model in Figure 7.2, we will now do a quick review of the Shingo Guiding Principles listed in Figure 7.3. More detail about these Guiding Principles is available in the *Shingo Model Handbook*, in the Shingo Discover Excellence course book, and most importantly in the Shingo workshops.

THE TEN PRINCIPLES

We will now do a quick review of each of the ten Shingo Guiding Principles. Starting with the first, lowest dimension we have Cultural Enablers, which focuses on defining the people relationship culture that should prevail within the enterprise. This dimension includes two Guiding Principles (pieces of these definitions are quoted directly from the *Shingo Model Handbook* and from the Shingo website):

> Respect every individual – Respect for every individual is manifested when organizations structure themselves to value each individual as a person and nourish their potential. When employees feel respected, they give not only their hands but also their minds and hearts. People want to be respected. They want to be engaged. They want to have meaning in their life and in their job.
>
> Lead with humility – Humility manifests itself when leaders seek out and value the ideas of others. Leaders should encourage employees to submit ideas, and they need to respond to suggestions positively, even if they are not implemented. Organizational and personal growth is enabled when leaders work to bring out the best in those they lead. When a leader is not principle based, a "blame culture" is created.

The second dimension, as seen in Figure 7.3, is the Continuous Improvement dimension and it includes five principles. An important footnote to this dimension is that there are some foundational tools (methodologies that TPS is built upon) that must be implemented prior to the successful use of any of the other dozens of TPS tools. These two foundational tools are 5S and standard work: 5S because you cannot improve a disorganized mess. This is a tool which is focused on organizational cleanliness and efficiency and includes:

Japanese Term	English Term	Explanation
Seiri	sort	Organize – Eliminate whatever is not needed. Separate needed tools, parts, and instructions from unneeded materials.
Seiton	set in order	Orderliness – Organize by neatly arranging and identifying parts and tools for ease of use.
Seiso	shine	Cleanliness – Clean the work areas.
Seiketsu	standardize	Standardize – Schedule regular cleaning and maintenance.
Shitsuke	sustain	Operationalize – Make 5S a way of life by forming the habit of always following the first four Ss.

The second foundational tool is standard work. This is important because, as we discussed in an earlier chapter, you cannot improve something that is not standardized. If everyone does a process differently, then it cannot be improved. The improved system would just become another way to execute an already confused process. The first step in Continuous Improvement is always to first 5S the processes and then to define standard work for the processes. Having accomplished that, we move on to the five Continuous Improvement principles.

Seek perfection – Seeking perfection means pursuing perfection. It is an ongoing, never-ending pursuit. Seeking perfection is looking at something beautiful and wanting to be like that. It is often referred to as searching for the True North. Seeking perfection has its focus on pursuing excellence.

Embrace scientific thinking – The first step of scientific thinking is to define standard work for the process being analyzed. Once the job is consistently done the same way, one can then take a closer look at failures or waste in that process. In scientific thinking, everyone in the enterprise looks at the problems objectively, realizing that it is the system and not the individual that is failing. It inspires repeated cycles of systems experimentation and improvement.

Focus on the process – All outcomes are consequences of a process or system. It is nearly impossible for even good people to consistently produce ideal results with a poor process, both inside and outside the organization. One needs to design systems that have considered the possibility of failure and are designed in such a way so as to make failure impossible. As discussed in previous chapters, the best systems are ones that make the right thing easier to do than the wrong thing.

Assure quality at the source – Do it right the first time. Do not pass poor quality forward. Stop the line if there is a quality failure. Another aspect of this principle is the Gemba concept, which drives one to "Go and Observe" the actual work at the location where the work is taking place.

Improve flow and pull – This is at the heart of TPS (Toyota Production System), incorporating the entire supply chain. The focus is on creating value and includes customers, marketing, production and operations, logistics, and vendors. It requires a study of the entire value stream and the elimination of waste at all the steps within the process.

The third dimension of the Shingo Model, as seen in Figure 7.3, is the Enterprise Alignment dimension, and it includes three principles:

Think systemically – What happens in one part of the process either improves or messes up what happens in other parts of the process. Thinking systemically means looking at the big picture. Everything is connected, and the better one understands these connections, the better they are able to make meaningful and goal-focused improvements.

Create constancy of purpose – This principle focuses on an unwavering clarity of why the organization exists, where it is going, and how it will get there. It aligns people's actions.

Create value for the customer – The focus of this principle is on creating value for all stakeholders. Organizations that fail to deliver both effectively and efficiently on this most fundamental outcome cannot be sustained over the long run.

At this point, you the reader, who has accepted the power found in the above set of ten foundational Shingo Guiding Principles, will be challenged with the question, "How do we get everyone within the enterprise to buy in?" The answer, unfortunately, is not easy. The answer comes in the form of education and training. Not necessarily the extensive training that you have received as you attend the six Shingo workshops. Fortunately, there is a short three-hour summary version of the Shingo Principle discussion that can be taken online. This summary is strictly to be used to give the line employee some background about the Shingo process, how it works, and what its goals are. To get the same level of thorough understanding that you the reader will have at the completion of the Shingo workshops would require attendance to all six workshops. This mini video summary is designed to facilitate buy-in which should help enterprises along their Shingo journey. You can get access to the video by contacting the Shingo Institute and getting their permission. The rules for accessing the video change from time to time, so it is best to work with the institute directly.

A second set of questions which the reader needs to consider is, "How can principles inform the design?" How do principles effect the continuous improvement implementation plan? How do they effect the sustainability of the cultural shift that is necessary for the long-term plan to work? Once again, the answer to these questions should be obvious. The principles are the foundation of the desired cultural shift. They orchestrate and define the culture we want to see within our organization. Because of this they inform the design of the implementation plan that we create. The design of the plan that we create for the implementation of our continuous improvement model is informed by the principles we choose to follow. And with a principle-based, culturally focused plan, we will create a sustainable cultural shift.

A third question that will come up is, "How can principles inform the selection of tools?" In a separate study on the Toyota Production System tools and the Continuous Improvement tools, the author learned that there are over 100 different tools available for facilitating change. Each principle has a tailored set of tools that can be used to help facilitate organizational change for a specific principle. The specific tools that are available for each principle are listed and discussed in the three Shingo workshops focused on the Guiding Principles. This question will also be addressed in more detail in a future chapter which describes the tools that are available and which correspond to each of the principles.

SUMMARY

In many ways, this chapter is one of the most important chapters of the book. If the Guiding Principles are not properly defined, and if they do not become the focus of the desired culture of the organization, then a culture of sustainable continuous improvement is not possible. Spot improvements may be achieved. But the larger picture of a focused cultural shift is not likely. The ten Shingo Guiding Principles should be treated as a guideline for the principles that are developed within your organization. A thorough understanding of these principles can be gained by attending the Shingo workshops, where the attendees go out and experience the principles in action. From this foundation, we can then move onward to other elements of the Shingo methodology.

> Treat people as if they were what they ought to be, and you help them become what they are capable of being.
>
> **Goethe**

8

Tools

Improvement usually means doing something that we have never done before.

The most dangerous kind of waste is the waste we do not recognize.

Know-how alone is not enough! You need to know-why! All too often, people visit other plants only to copy their tools and methods.

Shigeo Shingo

MORE REFLECTION

The importance of tools is fundamental to maintaining a sustainable bridge. Dr. Plenert was invited to a plant in Malaysia where they rebuilt alternators and starters for the US auto market. The plant manager was struggling. He explained,

> My competition, just down the street, has about the same number of employees, doing the same type of work, but they have about three times the output that we have in this plant. My employees work just as hard as theirs. Can you help me understand the difference?

Dr. Plenert answered, "Let's go out on the production floor and observe what is happening." He took the plant manager out on the production floor where they performed a Gemba or "go and observe" exercise. They stopped at one workstation and Dr. Plenert advised,

> Let us watch this person work. Let us pay attention to what they do and how they do it. And as we watch, let us time how much time they spend actually working on the product in proportion to how much time they spend moving the product around, doing setup, doing cleanup, etc.

What Dr. Plenert was doing was teaching the principle of value-added versus non-value-added time and the concept of waste.

After about 30 minutes of observation, the plant manager excitedly stated, "I get it. These people are working hard, but they are doing busywork. They are not creating value. I need to reorganize their work so they spend more time creating value and less time on non-value-added activities."

"Exactly," responded Dr. Plenert. "And who do you think would be the best at helping reorganize the work?"

The plant manager thought for a few seconds and then stated,

> Why the employees, of course. I need to get them thinking about how best to improve their work. I need them to understand what you just taught me. They can fix the problem themselves if they know what to watch out for.

In this case, the plant was so inefficient that a basic understanding of tools was critical. This shop needed to understand and implement tools like 5S, standard work, and Gemba, even before it was ready to work on higher level concepts like the Shingo Principles. This plant needed to literally "get off the ground" before they could successfully achieve a cultural transformation. However, understanding that the employees were the best source of information about how to make these improvements was also a critical insight and is a start down the road toward this transformation.

TOOLS

As mentioned, tools are often the place where most companies begin their continuous improvement journey. However, as we see in Figure 8.1, tools

FIGURE 8.1
A Tool-Based Architecture.

alone are not enough to achieve our goal of a continuous improvement environment leading to Enterprise Excellence.

Now we will transition to the Tool cube at the bottom of the Shingo Model (Figure 8.2). As we saw in our discussion of principles, each principle utilizes a set of tools in order to facilitate the necessary continuous improvements and systems changes that are desired and which will shift our culture toward our ultimate principle-based goal.

What the Shingo Institute has learned about tools is that this is unfortunately the necessary place where most enterprises start their continuous improvement journey. Organizations implement tools, like some version of Lean, or VSM (value stream mapping), or Six Sigma, and after a few years, they are left wondering why it does not stick. Why do work areas that have been improved tend to revert back to the traditional way of doing things? Why don't other areas of the organization get excited about the improvements that they have seen successfully implemented and use these tools throughout? Why is there no sustainability? Eventually, they realize that the foundation of lasting change is not in the tools; rather, it is in a shift in culture based on a set of principles. And once

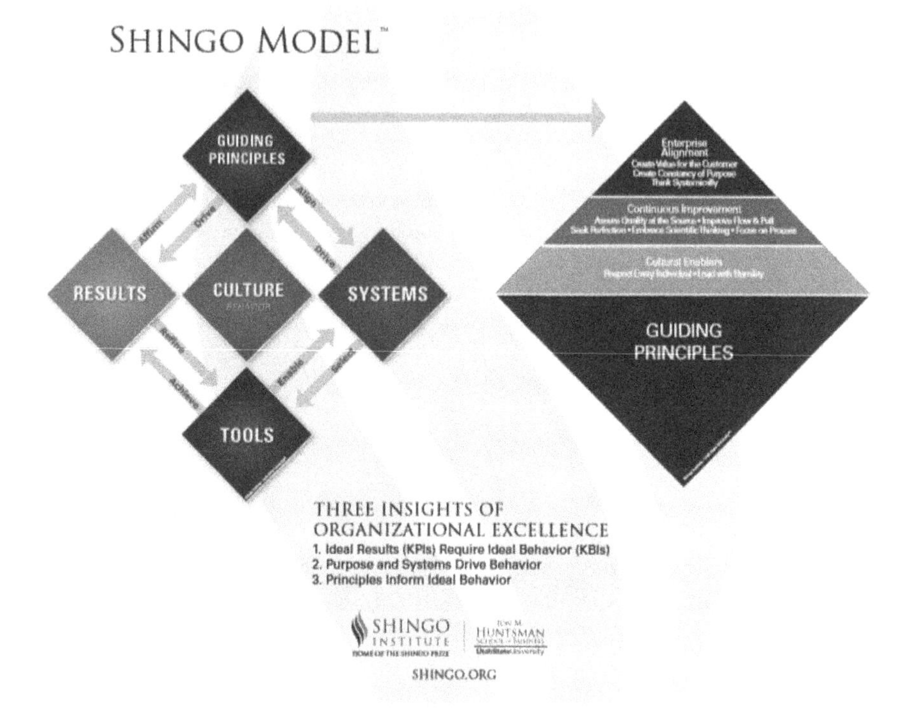

FIGURE 8.2
The Shingo Model.

an organization is founded upon principles, they then select the systems and the appropriate toolset that supports those principles. Reflecting on Figure 8.3, we tend to get the cart before the horse, thinking that we are somehow going to achieve excellence through the implementation of just a few magical tools.

Please do not misinterpret the message. Tools are critically important. But if they are not applied with a focus on principles, which in turn need to be the basis of the strategy, vision, and mission of the organization, then the random use of these tools can not only be ineffective, they may even be damaging to the principles. Think of it this way – tools are the nail, the principles are the hammer, and to drive in the nail which builds our enterprise, we need both of them to work together. Only then can we complete the bridge diagrammed in Figure 8.1. Only then do we close the gap.

The definition of a tool is, "A single device or item that accomplishes a specific task." As mentioned previously, there are over 100 "tools" available,

FIGURE 8.3
What Comes First?

and each has a specific purpose. But as we learned in the last chapter, there are two tools that are foundational and are critical to be applied before all others. We are restating what has been expressed previously in this chapter in order to add emphasis. These two tools are:

- 5S
- Standard Work

5S focuses on cleaning and organizing all your work areas. This is critical because you cannot improve the performance of a disorganized mess. If you spend all your time looking for tools, you are generating waste. The second critical tool, which is applied after 5S, is standard work. This is important because you cannot improve something that is not standardized. If there is no consistency in the process but instead where everyone does that same process differently, then improving one variation of the process still leaves other variations unimproved. The first steps in a plan for sustainable continuous improvement requires that we always first 5S the processes, and then define standard work for each of the processes. Having accomplished these steps, we can now move on to linking the organization's Guiding Principles to specific tools.

At this point, and as promised in the previous chapter, the author will now give the reader examples of some tools which can be applied to facilitate improvement to specific principles. It is critical to systematize (make it a standard behavior) the use of the right tools in connection to specific cultural behaviors that we are trying to shift in order to achieve sustainability. We have discussed the connection between tools and principles earlier. Here the author will list some relevant tools. (Detailed descriptions of each of these tools can be found in the book *Strategic Continuous Process Improvement: Which Quality Tools to Use, and When to Use Them*, by Gerhard Plenert, McGraw Hill, New York, 2012.)

Respect Every Individual

GEMBA
Acceptance Change Management Tools
Change Acceleration Process (CAP) Model
Kotter Change Model
Myers Briggs
Johari Window
Ladder of Inference
PAPT (Personality Aptitude Test)
Situational Leadership
Scan

Lead with Humility

GEMBA
Acceptance Change Management Tools
Change Acceleration Process (CAP) Model
Kotter Change Model
Myers Briggs
Johari Window
Ladder of Inference
PAPT (Personality Aptitude Test)
Situational Leadership
Scan

Seek Perfection

TPS – Toyota Production Systems
TQM – Total Quality Management
    Deming variation
    Crosby variation
    Juran variation
Process, Project, or Event Charter
Scan
Kaizen Events, Rapid Improvement Events (RIE)
PDCA – Plan Do Check Act
A3 Reporting
Root Cause Analysis
Value Stream Mapping
7 Wastes or 8 Wastes (including talent)
System Flow Chart
Swim-lane Chart
Spaghetti Chart
5S
Cellular Work Design
JIT – Just-in-Time
1 Piece Flow
Agile
Poka-Yoke
PQ Analysis
TPM – Total Product (Productive, Preventative or Production) Maintenance
Visual Workplace
DFM – Design for Manufacturability
SMED – Single-Minute Exchange of Die, Quick Changeover
Kanban
Jidoka
Standard Work
Brainstorming
Fishbone Charting
8 Step Problem Solving
VOC – Voice of the Customer
Gemba Walk – Go and See
Gap Analysis
Error Proofing/Mistake Proofing
SIPOC or COPIS
Affinity Diagrams
Concept Management

Embrace Scientific Thinking

TPS – Toyota Production Systems
Process, Project, or Event Charter
Scan
Kaizen Events, Rapid Improvement Events (RIE) – Includes Breakthrough (Kaikaku) improvement or small-step improvement (Kaizen)
PDCA – Plan Do Check Act or SDCA
A3 Reporting
Root Cause Analysis
Value Stream Mapping
7 Wastes or 8 Wastes (including talent)
System Flow Chart
Swim-lane Chart
Spaghetti Chart
Cellular Work Design
JIT – Just-in-Time
1 Piece Flow
Agile
Poka-Yoke
PQ Analysis
TPM – Total Product (Productive, Preventative or Production) Maintenance
Visual Workplace
DFM – Design for Manufacturability
SMED – Single-Minute Exchange of Die, Quick Changeover
Kanban
Jidoka
Standard Work
Fishbone Charting
8 Step Problem Solving
VOC – Voice of the Customer
Gemba Walk – Go and See
Gap Analysis
Error Proofing/Mistake Proofing
SIPOC or COPIS
Affinity Diagrams

Focus on the Process

TPS – Toyota Production Systems
Lean
Six Sigma
Process, Project, or Event Charter
Kaizen Events, Rapid Improvement Events (RIE)
Root Cause Analysis
Value Stream Mapping
7 Wastes or 8 Wastes (including talent)
System Flow Chart
Swim-lane Chart
Spaghetti Chart
5S
Cellular Work Design
JIT – Just-in-Time
1 Piece Flow
Agile
Poka-Yoke
PQ Analysis
TPM – Total Product (Productive, Preventative or Production) Maintenance
Visual Workplace
DFM – Design for Manufacturability
SMED – Single-Minute Exchange of Die, Quick Changeover
Kanban
Jidoka
Standard Work
Brainstorming
5 Whys
Fishbone Charting
8 Step Problem Solving
VOC – Voice of the Customer
Gemba Walk – Go and See
Gap Analysis
Error Proofing/Mistake Proofing
SIPOC or COPIS
Affinity Diagrams
Concept Management

Assure Quality at the Source

TPS – Toyota Production Systems
TQM – Total Quality Management
    Deming variation
    Crosby variation
    Juran variation
TQC – Total Quality Control
Root Cause Analysis
Agile
PQ Analysis
TPM – Total Product (Productive, Preventative or Production) Maintenance
Visual Workplace
Brainstorming
Fishbone Charting
Error Proofing/Mistake Proofing
Six Sigma
DMAIC (Define, Measure, Analyze, Improve and Control)
SQC – Statistical Quality Control
SPC – Statistical Process Control
Queuing Theory
DFSS (Design for Six Sigma)

Improve Flow and Pull

TPS – Toyota Production Systems
Lean
Root Cause Analysis
Value Stream Mapping
7 Wastes
System Flow Chart
Swim-lane Chart
Spaghetti Chart
5S
Cellular Work Design
JIT – Just-in-Time
Agile
Poka-Yoke
Visual Workplace
DFM – Design for Manufacturability

SMED – Single-Minute Exchange of Die, Quick Changeover
Kanban
Jidoka
Standard Work
Brainstorming
Fishbone Charting
8 Step Problem Solving
SWOT – Strengths, Weaknesses, Opportunities, Threats
VOC – Voice of the Customer
Gemba Walk – Go and See
Gap Analysis
Error Proofing / Mistake Proofing
SIPOC or COPIS
Pull Signaling
Affinity Diagrams

Think Systemically

TPS – Toyota Production Systems
TQM – Total Quality Management
 Deming variation
 Crosby variation
 Juran variation
Process, Project, or Event Charter
PDCA – Plan Do Check Act
Value Stream Mapping
System Flow Chart
Swim-lane Chart
Spaghetti Chart
TPM – Total Product (Productive, Preventative or Production) Maintenance
DFM – Design for Manufacturability
Standard Work
8 Step Problem Solving
SWOT – Strengths, Weaknesses, Opportunities, Threats
VOC – Voice of the Customer
Gemba Walk – Go and See
Gap Analysis
Concept Management

Create Constancy of Purpose

TPS – Toyota Production Systems
Process, Project, or Event Charter
TPM – Total Product (Productive, Preventative or Production) Maintenance
DFM – Design for Manufacturability
Standard Work
SWOT – Strengths, Weaknesses, Opportunities, Threats
VOC – Voice of the Customer
Concept Management

Create Value for the Customer

TPS – Toyota Production Systems
TQM – Total Quality Management
- Deming variation
- Crosby variation
- Juran variation

Dashboards
Scoreboards
KPIs
PQ Analysis
SWOT – Strengths, Weaknesses, Opportunities, Threats
VOC – Voice of the Customer

SUMMARY

This chapter has continued our climb up the ladder of continuous, sustainable improvement by describing how the use of tools supports the design of systems, which in turn focuses on principle-based results. At this point, you, the reader, should be starting to be able to piece together what is needed in order to achieve the level of Enterprise Excellence that this book hopes you are striving toward.

> The integrity of men is to be measured by their conduct, not by their professions.
>
> **Junius**

9

Results

The first problem in what we call improvement is to get a grip on the status quo. The most magnificent improvement scheme in the world will be worthless if your perception of the current situation is in error.

Shigeo Shingo

MORE TO REFLECT ON

Several years back, the author of this book, along with his co-author of a different book, was involved in an assessment experiment focused on identifying waste within an organization. The company they were working with at the time was Mitsubishi. The experiment proceeded as follows. Everyone was asked to log their activities for two weeks. They were guaranteed that no one would lose their job as a result of this activity. Employees recorded on a spreadsheet what activity they were engaged in and how much time they spent at this activity. At the end of the two-week period, the list was summarized, grouping repeated activities together.

Using the summarized list, employees were then asked, in the second column of the spreadsheet, to indicate the purpose of the activity. They needed to answer the question, "Why are you engaged in that activity?"

In the third column, they were asked to indicate the purpose of that previous purpose. What was the purpose of what was indicated in the second column?

In the next column, they were to indicate whether the second level purpose was:

Y – Yes this was an activity that satisfied the goals and objectives of the organization, which, in this case, were stated as "improving product quality" or "increasing customer satisfaction,"
N – No, this is an activity that does not satisfy the goals and objectives of the organization, or
? – Not sure if it does or does not satisfy the goals and objectives of the organization.

After the assessment, it was interesting to find an almost exact one-third split between each of the three responses (to within 1%). Employees were instructed to stop doing all the "N" items immediately. Employees suddenly found themselves with a one-third capacity increase. They were instructed to use this capacity boost to focus on "Y" activities and to do a better job at those, and not spend as much time on busywork as they had in the past. (For a detailed discussion of this experiment, go to the book *Making Innovation Happen: Concept Management through Integration*, DelRay Beach, Florida, St. Lucie Press, by authors Gerhard Plenert and Shozo Hibino.)

ASSESSMENTS

Reviewing Figure 9.1, the Shingo Model, we have considered all the elements of the model and discussed them several times in several ways. At this point, we will spend a little more time on the square on the left called "Results," which we discussed earlier when we talked about KBIs and KPIs. In order to look closely at this square, we need to start by considering the assessment element. An enterprise needs to constantly assess how the organization is doing with respect to ideal behaviors. There are numerous reasons for an assessment, the biggest one being that "We don't know what we don't know." There are several different types of assessment, but for the purpose of this chapter, we will eliminate any that do not directly and anonymously involve everyone throughout the organization. For example, surveying only the leadership will not give you

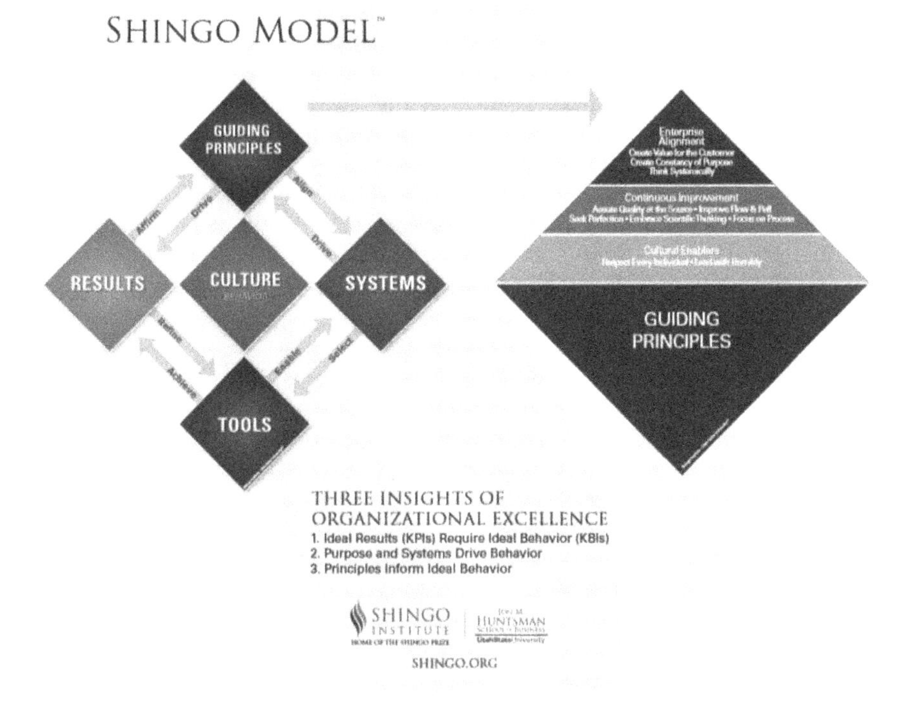

FIGURE 9.1
The Shingo Model.

a true evaluation of the culture of an enterprise. And it is the culture of the enterprise that we are attempting to transform.

Organizations will often focus on internal assessments, primarily because they consider these to be less expensive than external assessments. This has definite shortcomings in that the writer of the survey is prejudiced by their perspective and by the existing culture. Often the internal evaluator does not have a clear vision of what capabilities and opportunities lay beyond the organization and is therefore incapable of asking appropriate questions about the growth of the organization in comparison with the competition.

Another consideration that becomes important is in the definition of the assessment's objectives. Very few assessments focus specifically on principles and behaviors. They usually only ask about feelings and tools. And, as you already know, that only gets you half the way across the bridge. Without the correct, sustainable, continuous improvement culture being in place, it is difficult to meaningfully manage the performance of the tools.

THE ASSESSMENT TOOL – AN EXAMPLE

Understanding all my earlier points, let me give you some examples and suggestions on how to come up with a meaningful survey. As an example, I will use the assessment tool that the Shingo Institute offers. In Figure 9.2, we see the types of questions and their format. Questions should not have yes or no answers. They should be scalar, allowing for some level of ambiguity. The responders often do not see their world as either black or white. They see a lot of gray, and a well-constructed survey will allow for that.

This brings us to the Shingo Assessment Worksheet that we see in Figure 9.3. First, we will discuss the structure of the worksheet and then we will discuss how it is used. This is a tool that is used in the "Go and Observe" portion of the assessment process, as opposed to the earlier individual "survey" that we saw in Figure 9.2. In the first vertical column on the left edge of the page we see a dimension. As a reminder, there are three dimensions in the Shingo Model (reflect back on Figure 9.1 if needed).

- Cultural Enablers
- Continuous Improvement
- Enterprise Alignment

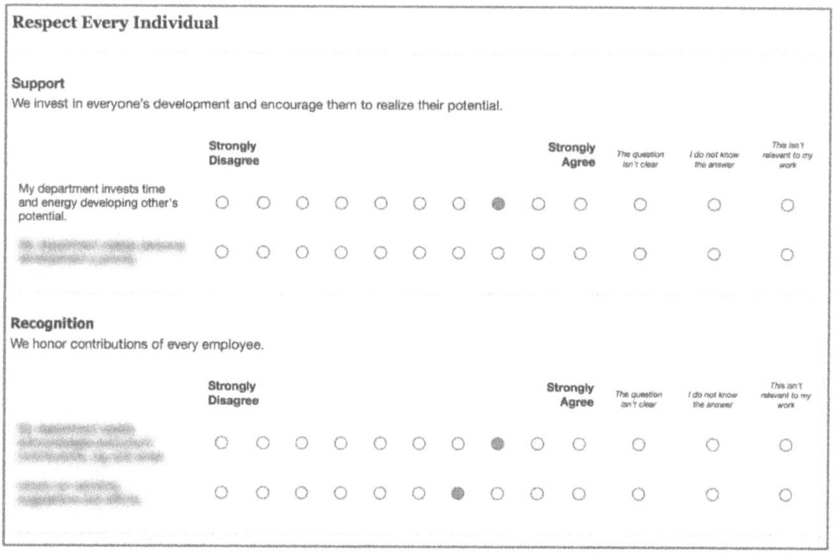

Respect Every Individual

Support
We invest in everyone's development and encourage them to realize their potential.

Strongly Disagree … Strongly Agree | *The question isn't clear* | *I do not know the answer* | *This isn't relevant to my work*

My department invests time and energy developing other's potential.

Recognition
We honor contributions of every employee.

Strongly Disagree … Strongly Agree | *The question isn't clear* | *I do not know the answer* | *This isn't relevant to my work*

FIGURE 9.2
The Shingo Insight Assessment.

Behavioral Maturity Scale						
Observations are measured against the key behavioral indicators using this cultural maturity scale. The scale incorporates five different characteristics as it relates to behavior. These characteristics are frequency, intensity, duration, scope and role. Descriptions indicate the top of each level (i.e. Barely = 20%).						
Systems	**Key Behavioral Indicators (KBI)**	Level 1 0-20% Barely matches KBI	Level 2 21-40% Lightly matches	Level 3 41-60% Somewhat matches	Level 4 61-80% Mostly matches	Level 5 81-100% Matches KBI
People Development						

Cultural Enablers

This is designed for training purposes and is not intended to be all inclusive or complete; it is not a checklist

FIGURE 9.3
The Shingo Insight Worksheet (example A).

Figure 9.3 is an example of how the Shingo assessment breaks out the left-hand column by Shingo Model Dimension. In Figure 9.3, the dimension example that we are working with is Cultural Enablers. If you attend the Cultural Enabler's Shingo workshop, you will study two Guiding Principles: Respect Every Individual and Lead with Humility. In that workshop, you will find "People Development" as one of the systems listed under the systems column as systems that have an influence on both of these principles. The objective of Figure 9.3 is to build out the KBIs that are expected under each system and to specifically define the type of performance that is expected.

The second large column in Figure 9.3 is the KBI column. In it we find a sample listing of the types of KBIs that can be expected in this system. Moving on to the last set of columns, we see five levels of performance rankings. These are used to evaluate the performance of the enterprise against the KBIs listed. This is again scalar, allowing the "Go and Observe" evaluator to assess the degree of compliance. These charts are extremely helpful in assessments, especially when performed by someone external to the organization. To get the completed and filled out worksheets would require attendance at the Shingo Guiding Principles workshops, which are the third, fourth, and fifth workshops in the Shingo series.

Behavioral Maturity Scale

Observations are measured against the key behavioral indicators using this cultural maturity scale. The scale incorporates five different characteristics as it relates to behavior. These characteristics are frequency, intensity, duration, scope and role. Descriptions indicate the top of each level (i.e. Barely = 20%).

	Systems	Key Behavioral Indicators (KBI)	Level 1 0-20% Barely matches KBI	Level 2 21-40% Lightly matches	Level 3 41-60% Somewhat matches	Level 4 61-80% Mostly matches	Level 5 81-100% Matches KBI
Cultural Enablers	Engagement						
	Environment, Health, Safety and Society (EHS²)						
	Measurement/ Motivation/ Recognition						

This is designed for training purposes and is not intended to be all inclusive or complete; it is not a checklist

FIGURE 9.4
The Shingo Insight Worksheet (example B).

Figure 9.4 shows three more categories of Cultural Enabler systems and similarly assesses them. All observations are measured against the key behavioral indicators using this cultural maturity scale. The scale incorporates five different characteristics as it relates to behavior. These characteristics are frequency, intensity, duration, scope, and role. Note that these assessment sheets are the same sheets that are utilized by examiners in a Shingo Prize assessment.

EXTERNAL ASSESSMENT

As mentioned earlier, external assessments are more expensive but also much more valuable than internal assessments. There are numerous reasons why, but one of them has already been highlighted:

- You do not know what you do not know. External assessments should introduce "experts" which have a broader background with experience in numerous industry sectors, thereby allowing them to make suggestions which would normally not even be on the radar of an internal assessment.

- An independent perspective as opposed to an ingrained corporate perspective offers the freedom to say things that may not be considered politically correct when viewed from inside the organization.
- A good, independent assessment will raise a different set of questions. It will identify opportunities that insiders did not even consider.
- A good, independent assessment should be able to identify the "Big Gaps" which an insider might miss. It is the "can't see the forest for the trees" syndrome. The external assessor should also be able to link the gaps to the enterprise priorities.
- An independent assessor should be able to prioritize the gaps using tools like the Impact/Effort Matrix and thereby help the enterprise focus their efforts accordingly (you'll learn more about this matrix in this chapter with Figure 9.6 or in Chapter 11 with Figure 11.1).

SHINGO INSIGHT

Now comes the sales pitch, but with a good reason. There is an external assessment tool available that focuses on assessing the culture of an organization with an emphasis on the Shingo priorities. This tool satisfies all the requirements of a clear and valuable external assessment while helping the organization refocus their efforts on the correct Shingo priorities. It helps them define which priorities are their strong points and which ones need more work.

Figure 9.2 shows the input tool for the Shingo Insight Survey tool. Figure 9.5 presents some of the highlights of the output of the Shingo survey.

The Shingo Insight tool is a simple methodology and is designed to be used on a regular basis, thereby allowing any organization to easily evaluate themselves frequently in order to assess their progress. It allows them to determine if the changes they are making to their systems are changing the desired behaviors, thereby impacting results. The Shingo Insight assessment is an organization's internal view of its culture, as opposed to most other third-party assessments. However, the Shingo look at the culture and KBIs of your organization, along with other assessment tools which look more at the KPIs of the organization, both of which offer valuable feedback on the performance of the enterprise.

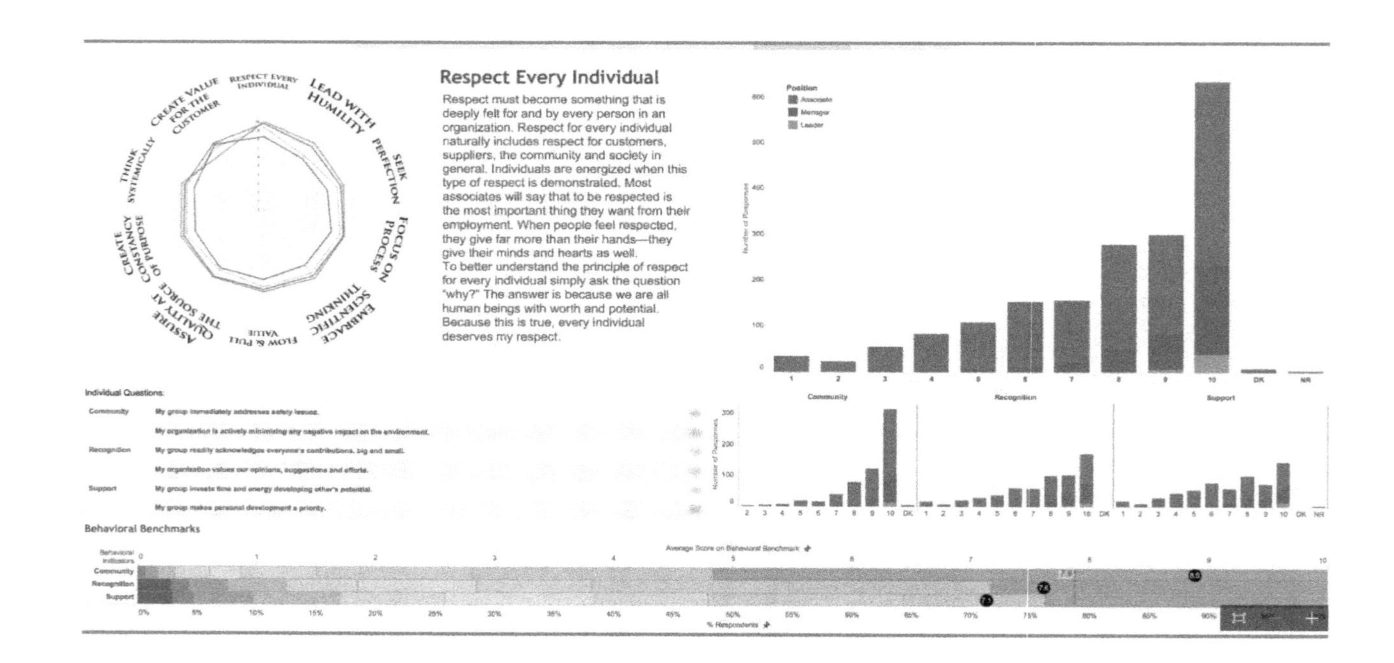

FIGURE 9.5
The Shingo Insight Output.

As organizations go through systems transformations, where improvements are anticipated, Shingo Insight helps them see if the people are following the new system and can measure the behavior changes brought about by the improvement. Organizations who choose to use the Shingo Insight tool are encouraged to complete the survey early so that they can use the initial survey as a benchmark to measure improvement.

Sample outputs from the Shingo Insight assessment tool are shown a Figure 9.5. Examples of the visible outputs include:

- The spider diagram (upper left) – The ten principles are listed around the circle chart, and by highlighting one of them, you can see your organization's assessment as it corresponds to that principle. The spider diagram shows the relative success of behaviors associated with each principle. Note the three lines across the bottom are colored in the actual document and these colored lines correspond to associate, manager, and leader levels. One of the interesting lessons learned from this chart is the disconnect between what leaders think is happening and what associates believe is happening. In this example, we see that associates have a much higher belief that the organization is "creating value for the customer" than what the leaders actually believe is the case.
- The heat diagram of behavioral benchmarks (the three lines across the bottom) – in the actual document the Green portion indicates success of observing good behaviors. Red (the "heat") demonstrates opportunities that might need improvement.
- Respondents by category – In the upper right-hand section we see the number of respondents who answered 10 versus 9 versus 8, and so on. This is broken down by the associate, the manager, and the leader.

It is easy to see how a repeat of this survey, on possibly an annual basis, would be an excellent indicator of how the enterprise is progressing in its growth as a Shingo Enterprise Excellent organization.

> In today's new business order, the spoils of corporate warfare belong not to the biggest companies, but to the quickest – those firms that consistently speed quality products or services to the marketplace and respond instantly to their customers' needs.
>
> **Philip R. Thomas**

THE SHINGO PRIZE

Reflecting back on the Shingo Prize, the assessment process that we have just reviewed is the methodology utilized during a Shingo Prize assessment (specifically Figures 9.3 and 9.4). The prize is much more than an award; it has become a standard for Enterprise Excellence. Organizations often go through the exercise of applying for the prize even though they never anticipate winning. They do it because they value having a team of experts tour and evaluate the performance of their facility. In this chapter, we will discuss the prize, the criteria for winning the prize, and some of the requirements behind applying for the prize.

The Shingo Prize is the world's highest standard for operational excellence. The Shingo Prize is awarded based on a complete assessment of an organization's culture and how well it drives world-class results. Shingo examiners focus on the degree to which the *Shingo Guiding Principles* of the Shingo Model™ are evident in the behavior of every employee. The examiners observe the behavior and determine the frequency, duration, intensity, and scope of the desired principle-based behavior. They also observe the degree to which leaders focus on principles and culture and managers focus on aligning systems to drive ideal behaviors at all levels. This focus is unique in the world and is the most rigorous way to determine whether an organization is fundamentally improving for the long term or just going through the motions of another flavor-of-the-month initiative.

A complete list of the impressive organizations that have joined the list of Shingo Prize winners can be found on the Shingo website at http://shingo.org/awards.

CHALLENGING FOR THE PRIZE

For details about how to challenge for the Shingo Prize, go to the Shingo Institute website at http://shingo.org/challengefortheprize. Scroll down the page to the second row of brown tabs and hit the button which says "Application Guidelines."

The details for challenging for the prize can be found on the website. In this chapter, we will give you a brief summary and some examples of what you will find there.

Assessment criteria – The Shingo assessment methodology is being embraced by organizations all over the world, without barrier to industry or geography. We have seen involvement expand far beyond its manufacturing roots into health care, government, and financial services. There are three levels of recognition in place to encourage organizations to engage and utilize the Shingo Model™ as early as possible in their cultural transformation. Organizations can be awarded the Shingo Prize, Shingo Silver Medallion, and Shingo Bronze Medallion. A third-party, non-biased assessment of your organization can provide a benchmark and eye-opening feedback that will accelerate your cultural transformation. The Shingo Prize is awarded to organizations that demonstrate a culture where principles of operational excellence are deeply embedded into the thinking and behavior of all leaders, managers, and associates. Performance is measured both in terms of business results and the degree to which business, management, improvement, and work systems are driving appropriate and ideal behavior at all levels.

Leadership needs to be strongly focused on ensuring the principles of operational excellence. These principles need to be deeply imbedded into the culture and regularly assessed for improvement. Managers are focused on continuously improving systems to drive behavior that is closely aligned with the principles of operational excellence. Associates are taking responsibility for improving not only their work systems but also other systems within their value stream. Understanding the "why" and not just the "how" has penetrated the associate level of the organization. Improvement activity has begun to focus on the enterprise as a whole.

Achievement reports are written by each applicant and tell the story of their transformation to operational excellence. The achievement report covers each dimension of the model and discusses the principles, systems, and tools that are evident and highlights the results they have produced. The achievement report, along with the survey, is used by members of the Shingo Board of Examiners to evaluate an applicant's eligibility to be awarded a site visit. Not all applicants will be awarded a site visit. And, not all organizations that receive a site visit will become award recipients.

> The Shingo principles, founded in logic and built over time, have assisted us in moving further towards operational excellence.
>
> **Pat Kealy, Business Excellence Manager**
> Abbott Vascular, Ireland

PRIORITIZATION

There are numerous prioritization tools, but one which we have found to work well is the Impact/Effort Matrix that you see on Figure 9.6. The Impact/Effort Matrix is a Lean tool used to prioritize projects and activities. At this stage, the focus on the Impact/Effort Matrix is more qualitative than quantitative. Objective methodology still needs to be applied as the project plan is outlined. But at this point, we are looking for a quick cut at prioritizing all the change activities that have previously been identified.

This is the tool the students would use for prioritizing which behavior and/or system should be worked on first. In filling out the matrix, all comparisons are relative to all the other activities that are being evaluated. For example, if we have identified ten activities, we should consider the relative impact that each activity will have on the overall goal/objective that we are trying to accomplish. Activities with a large impact should be mapped out toward the top of the diagram and activities with a low impact should be mapped near the bottom. Similarly, activities which require a large amount of effort, which means that a large amount of resources like labor and money will be needed, should be mapped toward the right side of the diagram, and activities which require very few resources will be mapped out toward the left.

We place a dot on the four-quadrant graph of Figure 9.6 for each of the activities, taking into consideration their relative impact and effort. Once all the activities have been mapped, we now know the relative importance of each activity. We know which activity should be performed first. As we plan which activity to work on, we diagonally work our way from the upper left-hand corner down to the bottom right-hand corner. Generally speaking, all the activities in the upper left-hand quadrant should be done first, then move on to the upper right-hand quadrant. Next, the bottom left-hand quadrant, and last of all, the bottom right-hand quadrant. It is not unusual to find that you never get around to the bottom right-hand activities because new activities will arise, and they will often take a higher priority than the bottom right-hand ones.

The prioritization step is extremely important in the Shingo workshops. It is utilized during almost any Lean or Six Sigma mapping exercise, where the students will be asked to engage in an individual exercise where they map all their planned activities out on an Impact/Effort Matrix. You, the

Behavioral Benchmarks will be subjectively prioritized by the team to identify the impact and effort priorities.

The Behavioral Benchmarks in the Upper Left Hand quadrant will receive the most immediate focus, followed by the Upper Right Hand and Lower Left Hand quadrants.

At this stage the focus in the Impact/Effort matrix is more qualitative than quantitative. Objective methodology still needs to be applied.

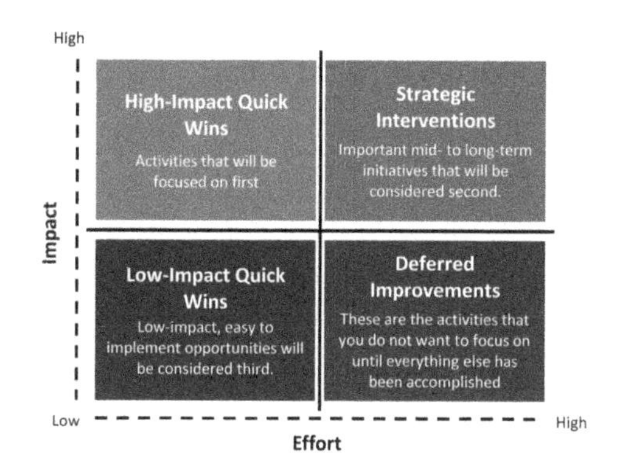

*The **Impact/Effort Matrix** is a lean tool used to prioritize projects and activities.*

FIGURE 9.6
Impact/Effort Matrix.

reader, should also engage in this exercise. Use the following steps to plan your own prioritization activity:

1. Identify a system or systems in your organization in which there is a gap between current and ideal behavior.
2. Identify the activities (changes) that will need to be accomplished in order to move from the current to the ideal behavior. Choose a system(s) that you propose to design or redesign and what are the steps necessary in this redesign.
3. Use the Impact/Effort Matrix to prioritize the activities (changes) under consideration.
4. What are you going to do first? Second? etc.

This exercise starts to "bring home" the connectivity between systems and behaviors within the participant's organizations. At this point, the reader should start to focus on their own organization, rather than just some generic sample organization. What are the behaviors within your organization that are incorrect? And what are the connected/related systems? What should the ideal behavior look like? And how can we "move the needle" within your organization in order to get closer to that point? The reader should start to become comfortable with what they need to be doing next within their own organizations.

MORE ABOUT RESULTS

Referring back to Figure 9.1, the "Results" cube is highlighted on the left side of the Shingo Model. The ultimate goal for an enterprise is results, which include the vision, the mission, the strategy, the KPIs by which the outside world will use to evaluate your enterprise's success, and the KBIs that will be used internally to motivate employees' performance. Hence, KPIs only reside in "Results," but KBIs reside everywhere throughout the organization and are specifically defined and implemented through "Systems."

Results need to be approached and achieved through KBIs rather than KPIs. KBIs lead, whereas KPIs report. KBIs are leading indicators and KPIs are lagging indicators. Note that KPIs rest only with results, but KBIs influence the priorities throughout the organization. KBIs define the culture and monitor the performance of the principles that we have put in place as the ideals for our organization.

We have learned how systems drive behaviors, which influence KBIs, and through them directly affect KPIs and results. So, what are the ideal results? The Shingo Institute definition of ideal results is:

> Ideal Results are actions that are aligned with enterprise goals and objectives, and which are both excellent and sustainable. They demonstrate continuous improvement over time.

At this point, we would like to share the testimonials of several employees from one of the Shingo Prize winners, Abbott Vascular, Cashel Road, Clonmel, Tipperary, Ireland. This is the transcript of a video presented during the Shingo Build Excellence workshop.

> Bozena Markowska, Assembler
>
> Abbott is a global healthcare company devoted to improving life through the development of products and technologies that span the breadth of healthcare.
>
> **Robert Mulkerrins, Manufacturing Group Lead**
>
> Here in Clonmel, Ireland, we are a center of excellence in the manufacturing of medical devices.
>
> **William Boxwell, Site Director**

We are honored to receive the Shingo Prize for Operational Excellence. The Shingo Model helped us create a long term vision and with it, discover more effective ways to collaborate and improve on everything we do.

Pauline Hanley, Director, Quality

Our quality policy, "Built as if intended for family," reinforces our focus of putting the people who are treated with our products first. The Shingo methodology has helped us to further strengthen our quality metrics, ensuring we continue to provide the highest quality products to our customers around the world. As well as continuous improvement in our quality metrics, we have delivered a double digit reduction in product unit costs. As part of our six-sigma program, 80% of all our employees are green or black belt certified.

Grainne Mason, Operations Supervisor

We use a 14-step process to drive for transformational change. For example, a recent project has delivered 38% increase in productivity.

Mike Tarrant, Business Excellence Manager

We always strive to improve every facet of what we do. For example, we improved our lead time from manufacturing to the customer by 85% over the last six years. Benchmarking has helped us develop a leaner enterprise through greater flow and pull within our value systems and ultimately the best product for the people who our products reach. It's no longer good enough to be good, we need to be great.

Alan Meehan, Director, HR

An important part of achieving operational excellence was improving our two-way communication. Key to this was our continuous improvement huddles. These huddles empower our employees to develop creative solutions to challenging operational issues.

Carol Smyth, Assembler

These huddles are a great way for teams to come together and try to figure out how we can do things better. For example, our team developed a piece of tooling to successfully help resolve an issue that we faced on the assembly line, therefore improving line output.

William Boxwell, Site Director

> The heart of our site is our employees. It has been a privilege for all of us to be a part of this operational excellence journey. The Shingo Model will continue to be our guide to sustain a culture of excellence so we continue to be better today than we were yesterday.

Let us briefly reflect back on the messages that we learned from these testimonials.

- What was the central message of the video? There are several, but what is important is the message that resonated with you, whether it is the people focus or the quality focus, etc.
- What two or three things did the video highlight which are important to you?
- What are some specific things you can take back with you when you get back to work?
- What will you do differently? This is the most important question. If you do not change anything, if you did not learn anything, if these testimonials did not trigger some ideas in your mind, then they were all a waste.

> A company's values – what it stands for, what its people believe in – are crucial to its competitive success.
>
> **Robert Hass, CEO**
> Levi Strauss & Co.

10

Culture

If we want to achieve improvement, we must first have the mental flexibility to believe that even though there is only one summit, there are many paths we can tread to reach it. If we adamantly think that the current methods are the best and no other means are possible, improvement ideas will never emerge.

Shigeo Shingo, *Kaizen and the Art of Creative Thinking*

ONE MORE REFLECTION

Dr. Gerhard Plenert, the author of this book, was involved in the relocation of a transmission production plant from Jackson, Michigan, to Queretaro, Mexico. The objective was to take advantage of the labor cost reduction that they expected to get from the cheaper Mexican labor. Looking at the KPIs, the move was a success. The cost of operation for the plant was significantly less than the previous plant in Michigan. However, there are some KPI considerations that were not accounted for.

1. The cost of transporting materials back and forth from Michigan to Mexico was allocated to overhead, not to the cost of operating the new facility.
2. The cost of the in-process transit inventory, which previously was a few days, was now measured in weeks, and that cost was also allocated to overhead.

3. The total manufacturing lead time for the finished vehicle had significantly increased because of the transport time.
4. Occasional border delays also increased the lead time.
5. One of the brass gears in the transmission had to be cut with extreme precision, and the machining in Mexico did not meet the required specs, causing a large amount of waste. The decision was made to have the gear produced in Japan and then transported to Mexico to be installed into the transmission. All of these additional costs were also allocated to overhead.

The KPIs said that moving the plant was a smart move. But if all the overhead that was specific to the new location was added back to the Mexico plant, the cost of the new facility was higher than the cost of the old facility in Michigan.

The message is simple, "Don't trust the KPIs without looking at the big picture."

> What luck for rulers that men do not think.
>
> **Adolf Hitler**

ASSESSING CULTURE

This is an exciting chapter in that it offers up one of the most valuable tools in the Shingo Institute arsenal. We start by looking at Figure 10.1, which is a critical notes worksheet, and which is used for external assessments and also in the internal "Go and Observe" (Gemba) process.

In reviewing this worksheet, we start by explaining how each of the boxes on the worksheet is used.

- Area – The physical area, department, operation, etc., that is under study.
- Focus – The principle, system, behavior, etc., that we are studying with the "Go and Observe" exercise.
- Round – The first, second, third, etc., time that we are engaging in this specific "Go and Observe" exercise.

Assessment Notes

AREA:	FOCUS:	ROUND:

IDEAL BEHAVIOR	OBSERVED BEHAVIOR
1	1
2	2
3	3
4	4
5	5
6	6
7	7
8	8
9	9
10	10

SYSTEMS	SYSTEM GENERATED BEHAVIORS

KEY QUESTIONS
1
2
3
4
5
6
7
8
9
10

Behavior - can be observed, described and recorded.

Ideal Behavior - Actions that create outcomes that produce results and that are both excellent and sustainable.

FIGURE 10.1
Assessment Notes.

- Ideal behavior – A behavior is an event that can be observed, described, and recorded. An ideal behavior is an event or action that creates outcomes which produce results and that are both excellent and sustainable.
- Observed behavior – The resulting behavior that occurred as you observed the event.
- Systems – The system(s) under study.
- Systems generated behaviors – The behaviors that are directly linked and are outputs from the system(s) under study.
- Key questions – Questions that need to be answered during the "Go and Observe." We should try to make these questions answerable by observation whenever possible, rather than by interviews which tend to disrupt the workflow and the answers are often idealized.

The process of using this form is systematized as follows:

1. In a team meeting, discuss what behavior we are trying to create or modify. Then discuss what systems you initially feel are linked

to this behavior. It is not unusual to discover during the "Go and Observe" that the system you thought was causing the behavior is not the culprit and that you need to be studying a different system, or possibly even multiple systems. As a team you should fill in:
   - Area
   - Focus
   - Round
   - Ideal behavior
   - Systems
   - Key questions
2. Perform the first round of the "Go and Observe" Gemba, which requires a minimal amount of talking and a maximum amount of observing. A good first round Gemba will take a minimum of 30 minutes and could possibly run several hours, depending on the complexity and length of the process under observation. During the "Go and Observe," fill out the following sections of the worksheet.
   - Observed behavior
   - Systems generated behaviors
3. Reconvene as a team and discuss your leanings. Compare notes between team members. The first round will not be sufficient, and more rounds will be needed. Each time, as you go out in future "Go and Observe" Gembas, repeat the same process, and after each observation, reconvene and discuss your learnings until the entire team feels confident that they have a thorough understanding of the systems and the corresponding behaviors. Only then are you ready to start discussing changes to or a replacement of the existing system. One of the biggest causes of failure in this process is "jumping the gun" by thinking you already know the answer, thinking you already know what needs to be changed, without having a clear and thorough understanding of the big picture and of the interactive effects of what is being changed.

Creativity is intelligence having fun.

Albert Einstein

THE SHINGO BEHAVIORAL BENCHMARK ASSESSMENT WORKSHEET

As promised earlier in this chapter, we are now going to tell you about one of the most valuable tools that you will find yourself using over and over again in your Shingo journey. We are now going to show you how the Shingo Behavioral Benchmark Assessment Worksheet looks (the full/filled-out worksheet is given to the attendees of the various Shingo workshops). This worksheet is something you can develop internally within your organization, and even if you have the full Shingo version, you should personalize it to your specific enterprise. The Shingo worksheets that you would get during the workshops are intended to be suggestions and examples, not the know-all and end-all answers to this process. Using this worksheet gives you a critical tool that will help you identify weaknesses within your organization and will facilitate your study and improvement in the areas of your organization's weaknesses.

We begin building our understanding of the Shingo Behavioral Benchmark Assessment Worksheet by looking at Figure 10.2, which shows

Shingo Assessment Worksheet

	Behavioral Benchmarks	Core Ideal Behaviors	Systems	Key Behavioral Indicator (KBI)	Potential Questions
Respect Every Individual	1.1 **Support**				
	1.2 **Recognition**				
	1.3 **Community**				

This is designed for training purposes and is not intended to be all inclusive or complete; it is not a checklist

FIGURE10.2
Assessment Worksheet.

the headings and breakdown of the worksheet without showing any of the actual content. We will now discuss the worksheet in detail.

Let us work our way around the headings that are on the sheet. Then we will discuss how it is best utilized. Draw one out and start filling it out specific to your organization. Do not wait for the course to get the Shingo version of this sheet. It's just an example anyway. Create your own version of the worksheet that is specific to your company.

- Along the left-hand side of the worksheet page, listed vertically, is the principle that we are looking at. In this example, the principle is "Respect Every Individual."
- The behavioral benchmarks that correspond to the principle are then listed in the first large column. In this case, there are three behavioral benchmarks that correspond to "Respect Every Individual." These benchmarks are discussed in detail during the Cultural Enablers workshop, and to go through them here would take another book by itself. This book assumes you understand the benchmarks and how they relate to the principle being discussed.
- The next column in the spreadsheet is titled "Core Ideal Behaviors," and this includes examples of ideal behaviors that correspond to the benchmark being discussed. We stress that the Shingo versions are "examples" and not to be considered all-inclusive. In the Shingo Institute experience, we have learned that every time we go out on a site visit, we learn of more ideal behaviors. This spreadsheet is dynamic, ever growing, and ever changing, especially as additional industry sectors are introduced. And all possible cases cannot be considered. Therefore, consider all the information in the Shingo versions of these spreadsheets to be examples and not a checklist of any type. Start immediately by creating your own version of these worksheets.
- The next column in the spreadsheet is labeled "Systems." In this case, we would see examples of the types of systems that tie to these behaviors. At this point, you can start seeing the value of these spreadsheets. If you reflect back to Figure 10.1, you saw the need for identifying the systems that need to be studied during your "go and observe" exercise, and this spreadsheet is designed to help you get started, identifying the systems that would exist within your organization.

- The next column is labeled "Key Behavioral Indicator (KBI)," and this is also important as you look to redesign systems that are causing behaviors that are not ideal.

At this point, you should be excited about seeing how all of these different elements connect together, starting with behavioral benchmarks, and how they tie to Core Ideal Behaviors, and how there are Systems that tie to these behaviors, and lastly how there are KBIs that can be used to monitor the success of each behavior.

- The last column in this spreadsheet is labeled "Potential Questions." Once again we need to stress that these would be examples and are not to be considered all-inclusive. However, considering these questions helps us fill out the bottom portion of the worksheet in Figure 10.1. It gives us ideas, and then we need to customize these ideas to the specific environment that we will be studying.

Now that we understand all the columns of the spreadsheet in Figure 10.2, let us consider the process for using these sheets in conjunction with the use of the worksheet shown in Figure 10.1. The process should go something like:

1. Get together as a team and select a principle that you would like to focus on and which you feel requires improvement within your organization. This may be the result of some undesirable behavior within the organization that your team would like to change. Or it may be some principle or behavior that management would like to see strengthened. What are the organizational weaknesses that your team needs to focus on?
2. Prioritize the areas of weakness and select the one(s) that your team is going to focus on. Do not overextend yourself by trying to solve everything at once. It is better to do a good job on adjusting a few behaviors, then to do a poor job focusing on too much. This prioritization may require a confirmation with management.
3. As a team, tie down the principle and behavioral benchmark(s) that you will be focusing on and fill out the worksheet (Figure 10.1) that we discussed earlier in this chapter.

4. Go through a repetitive cycle of "Go and Observe(s)," as we discussed earlier in this chapter, until you fully and completely understand the behaviors and the systems that are causing those behaviors. Rarely will your first impressions be correct. Do not jump to conclusions too quickly.
5. Work together as a team to make sure you all agree on the lessons learned from the "Go and Observe," and then, when you are in agreement, go to work on redesigning the systems that are causing these behaviors.

At this point, you have the secret sauce that is critical in adjusting organizational behavior and driving it closer toward what you consider to be the ideal behaviors. As you saw in the last chapter, rarely do you jump to the final successful solution in one step. It often takes multiple steps to achieve success. Additionally, what is considered a success today may not be considered success several years down the road. Achieving Enterprise Excellence is an iterative, ongoing, continuous improvement process that never ends.

Worth noting is that the worksheets in Figures 9.3 and 9.4 and Figures 10.1 and 10.2 are the same worksheets that are used during the site evaluations that occur when examiners do the site visit of a candidate for the Shingo Prize.

DOES THE RIGHT CULTURE EXIST?

Referring back to Figure 8.3, which comes first? Tools or Culture? Most companies start with tools and, realizing that they are not sustainable on their own, introduce a cultural shift. In the end, the two need to work together. You need both pillars in order to hold up the bridge in Figure 10.3. Either one by itself is not sustainable.

A key foundational goal of the Shingo Model is to create a culture of sustainable continuous improvement. Traditional Lean and Six Sigma applications of the Toyota Production Model have suggested that success is found in the tools. But the Shingo Institute has learned the hard way, as did Toyota, that tools only give us half of the bridge to success, that we can see in Figure 10.3. The tools give us the spot improvements, but

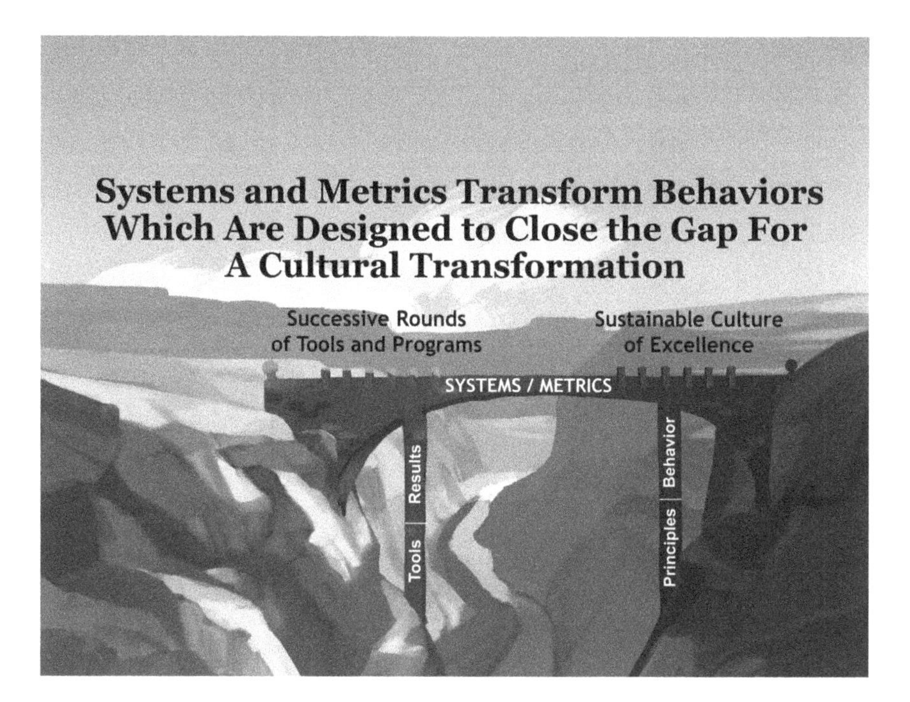

FIGURE 10.3
The Shingo Bridge to Success.

these improvements are only sustainable when a principle- and behavior-based cultural shift occurs throughout the organization and at all levels within the organization. Using the Shingo Principles, we learn how to create a sustainment-based culture that will eventually lead us to the level of Enterprise Excellence that we all desire.

Let us take another look at the Shingo Model in Figure 10.4. Appropriately, at the very heart of the model is Culture. All the other elements, Guiding Principles, Systems, Results and Tools, work together toward one central purpose, which is:

> creating and sustaining a culture of continuous improvement.

If this does not exist, the others will not sustain! They will not stay focused! Tradition will eventually take over once again, and all the other gains, no matter how wonderful they seemed at the time, will go away. Hence, the only true and sustainable way to achieve this goal is through the tried and tested Shingo methodology. This methodology is the only way to achieve

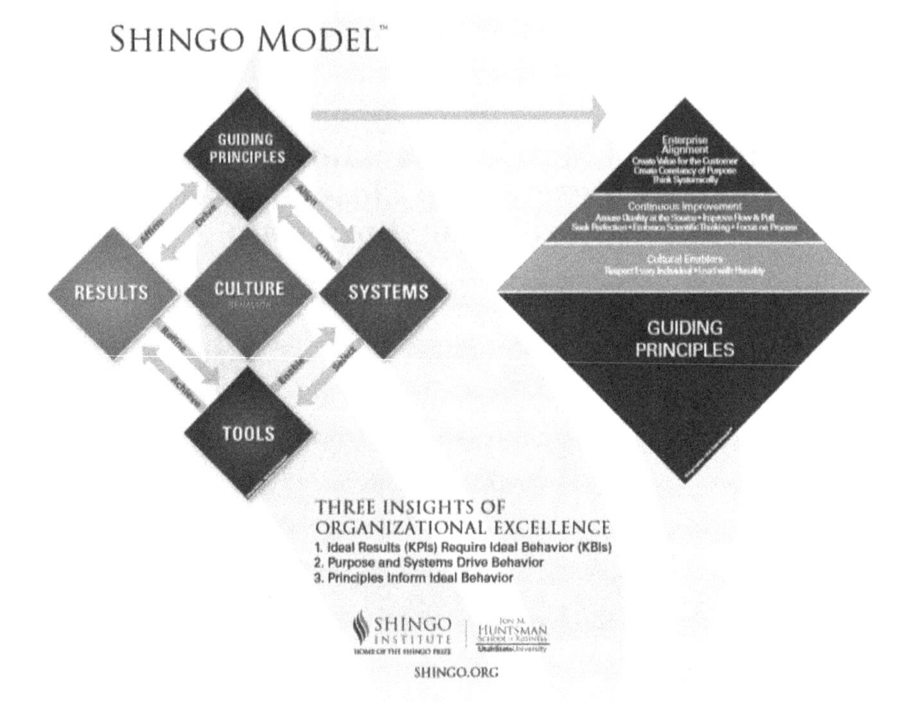

FIGURE 10.4
The Shingo Model.

what Toyota and other similar companies have achieved. No piece of the bridge can get you across the canyon on it is own and by itself.

SUMMARY

This chapter utilizes the learnings about systems that you gained in the last chapters and helps build a structure for continuous improvement that will help you achieve Enterprise Excellence. It discusses the elements of culture and how cultural status can be assessed. It shows the worksheets used in the assessment process in conjunction with the "Go and Observe" activities. This chapter, in conjunction with the last chapter, mentions the criticality of the worksheets in internal and external assessments, including the Shingo Behavioral Benchmark Assessment Worksheet. These worksheets, completely filled out, are given to you as part of the

Shingo workshops and will become a critical example for you as you create your own, customized worksheets and as you work your way across the bridge to cultural sustainability.

> A cardinal principle of total quality escapes too many managers: you cannot continuously improve interdependent systems and processes until you progressively perfect interdependent, interpersonal relationships.
>
> **Stephen R. Covey**

Part III

Bringing It Home

11

Making It Actionable

Are you too busy for improvement? Frequently, I am rebuffed by people who say they are too busy and have no time for such activities. I make it a point to respond by telling people, look, you'll stop being busy either when you die or when the company goes bankrupt.

Shigeo Shingo

ANOTHER REFLECTION

NUMMI was a joint venture between General Motors in the United States and Toyota from Japan. There were a lot of struggles in blending the two management styles, and there have been a lot of books published about the US perspective of this merger. In the Discover Excellence workshop, the first in the Shingo series of workshops, we had a case study on the NUMMI implementation.

One interesting story that came out of this implementation occurred when a Japanese executive came to visit the NUMMI plant in the San Francisco Bay Area. He was walking on a plant tour with an American executive, and he asked him, "What problems are you having in the plant?"

The GM executive's response was, "We're not having any problems. Things have been running very smoothly."

The Toyota executive turned to the American, shook his finger at him, and said, "No Problem is Problem!"

The job of the leader is to search for opportunities for improvement. It is the leader's job to focus continuously on making things better. His job is to search for systems and behavior shortcomings. If the leader/executive is not working on a problem, then he or she is simply not doing their job. Hence, "No Problem is Problem."

If you want to read a detailed account of the NUMMI implementation from the Japanese/Toyota perspective, rather than the dozens of books written from a Western perspective (which aren't very useful because, looking at GM, they didn't work), take a look at the book *Toyota's Global Marketing Strategy: Innovation through Breakthrough Thinking and Kaizen*, Taylor and Francis Group, CRC Press, 2017, and authored by Kouichiro Noguchi, a former director of Toyota, Shozo Hibino, the author of the "Breakthrough Thinking" series, and Gerhard Plenert, the author of this current book.

PREPARE TO MOVE FORWARD

We start this chapter with a review and a little reflection on what we have learned up to this point. The reader needs to ask themselves the following questions:

- How have things changed for you since you started reading this book? Specifically, how has your perspective changed?
- What are the two or three things you have learned?
- What are some specific things you can do immediately when you get back to work?
- Who will you share these learning points with when you get back to work?
- What will you do differently?
- The ultimate question is, "What will you change within your organization?"

Having completed a little reflection, we now need you to do a little preparation. Gather the following materials within your organization so that you are now ready to proceed with a discussion of the next steps. The things you need are:

A. Corporate strategy/vision/mission/Guiding Principles documents if you have them (not having them tells you something too)

B. Systems lists specific to your organization (something you may have to create)
C. Survey analysis results (from an externally performed assessment process like the ones mentioned in this book)

These three items are critical as we move forward to do a meaningful review of the performance within your organization. We are searching for performance gaps, and these three tools will help us drill down on those gaps.

Additionally, in a previous chapter, we had an extensive discussion of tools that are critical to the successful implementation of a continuous improvement process. The two tools that were highlighted as critical when we start a process of this type and which are strongly emphasized were:

D. 5S
E. Standard Work

Unfortunately, these requirements can also be a roadblock, preventing us from moving forward. For example, if standard work is not in place, we cannot improve a process or a system that is inconsistent in the way it is executed. Similarly, if the corporate strategy and vision are not in place, we would be trying to shoot an arrow at a target that does not exist. We need to know where our bull's eye is located in order to aim for it.

Hence, if items A through E above are not in place, we need to stop right here and address these shortcomings first before we can successfully move forward with the creation of a plan for continuous improvement. We cannot achieve excellence if we do not know what excellence looks like for us.

CREATING A PLAN

At this point, we are going to assume that all the pieces listed in A through E above are in place and we are ready to create a plan for execution. In this chapter, we will work through an exercise that will help us develop an improvement plan for one specific area of the organization. We are limiting our scope for several reasons, the first being that you simply do not have the resources to do everything at once. The second reason is that, at this point, we are trying to develop an example plan and once you understand how that plan works you will be able to replicate that same process as you facilitate improvements in other parts of the organization. Trying to do everything at once tends to drive chaos throughout the organization. It is not healthy for you or your company.

To start this process, let us make sure we all agree with the goal that we are trying to accomplish:

> GOAL: To study the existing systems / behaviors and create a plan to transform the systems with a focus on reinforcing ideal behaviors that support our Guiding Principles.

Agreeing with this goal, we move forward with a two-stage exercise. This exercise should be executed as a team rather than as one lone individual. The team perspective has a synergistic effect where the various perspectives allow us to learn more and offer us more insights than we would gain individually on our own.

The first part of this two-step process involves the following steps:

A. Identify areas of focus. There are several tools that can be utilized to identify this focus. For example:
   a. The corporate strategy/vision document can be used to identify areas of weakness where we feel the organization is faltering. We identify the principles that would support this element of the vision and start by looking at potential performance gaps in that area.
   b. Behavioral benchmarks/systems lists specific to your organization will be utilized. These should give you a jump start on performance gaps that were previously identified.
   c. The Shingo Insight survey analysis or any other survey analysis is also designed to help you focus on performance gaps and disconnects between the various levels of the organization. In the survey, you should be pointed directly at the principles and behavioral benchmarks that are associated with the disconnects that are occurring.
B. Select an area of focus. Do not overextend or your chance of success will be reduced, and early failures can destroy the improvement momentum for the entire organization.

C. Review the systems connected with the area of improvement that you have selected, and within your team create a consolidated list of associated systems which have an effect on the selected area of your organization. You have identified the gaps or areas of disconnect. Now we need to see which systems may be creating these gaps and take a closer look at each of them.
D. Prioritize the consolidated list of organizational systems using an Impact/Effort Matrix on Figure 11.1. Which systems do we feel have the most significant impact on the gap, and which would require the least amount of effort to change? This prioritization will change as we learn more about the behaviors and the associated systems, and as we work our way toward a plan for corrective action.

   As a review, behavioral benchmarks on the chart you create will be subjectively prioritized by the team to identify the impact and effort of each of the gaps/priorities. The behavioral benchmarks in the upper left-hand quadrant will receive the most immediate focus, followed by the upper right-hand and lower left-hand quadrants. At this stage, the focus in the Impact/Effort Matrix is more qualitative than quantitative. Objective methodology still needs to be applied once budget approval is needed in order for the project/effort to move forward.

Behavioral Benchmarks will be subjectively prioritized by the team to identify the impact and effort priorities.

The Behavioral Benchmarks in the Upper Left Hand quadrant will receive the most immediate focus, followed by the Upper Right Hand and Lower Left Hand quadrants.

At this stage the focus in the Impact/Effort matrix is more qualitative than quantitative. Objective methodology still needs to be applied.

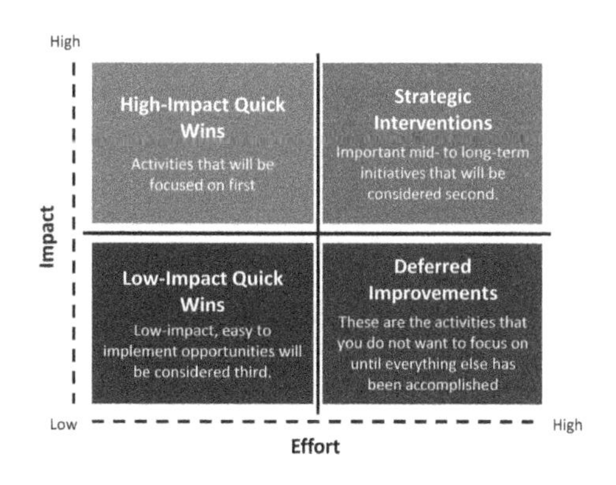

The ***Impact/Effort Matrix*** *is a lean tool used to prioritize projects and activities.*

FIGURE 11.1
Impact/Effort Matrix.

E. Why are you choosing these systems as the ones that need change? This is a question that you will need to be able to answer during your executive "Go and Observe" meetings later in this workshop.
F. Select three or four high-impact/low-effort systems for further study/projects/activities.
G. Go on a "Go and Observe" to focus on the systems (and corresponding behaviors) that you have selected. Remember the points that were stressed earlier. The "Go and Observe" is about "observing," not about getting a tour of the process. And it should be at least 30 minutes and closer to 120 minutes (depending on the process and how long each cycle of the process takes) if you are expecting to get a clear understanding of the behaviors and associated systems.

Here are some further thoughts about the "Go and Observe" stage of this process since this is the critical learning stage. All the rest of what we do is a desk exercise. The "Go and Observe" is where we find out what reality looks like. At this point, you would need to have filled out the sheet in Figures 11.2 and 11.3 as a team. Then, using the sheets, the team should go to one of the designated locations and work on studying the selected systems.

As a review from previous "Go and Observe" exercises, we should remember that the purpose of this exercise is to make sure participants understand that you cannot improve something you don't understand. As you go through the exercise, you need to look for subsystems/side systems/etc., that influence each other and influence the area that you are focused on. It is important to make sure the following information is recorded into the notes because it will become important later when you consider various alternatives:

- What systems did I study?
- What behaviors did I observe?
- What gaps did I observe that were not ideal?
- What are my recommendations?
- What is my plan to design/redesign the system?

These last two points are analyzed and discussed as a team when you reconvene after the "Go and Observe."

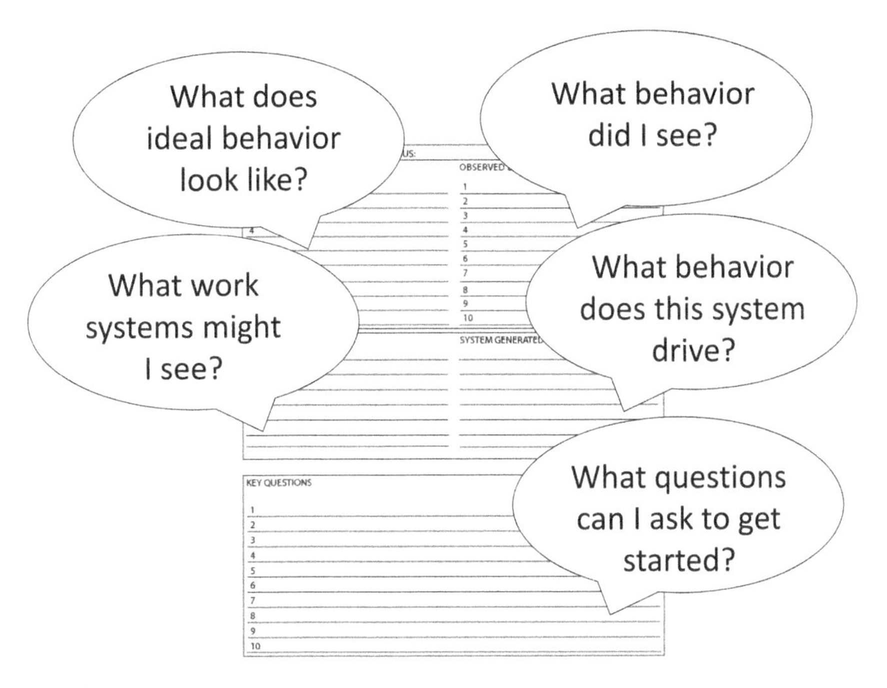

FIGURE 11.2
Assessment Worksheet.

The deliverable at the end of the "Go and Observe" exercise should be an A3 (Figure 11.4 – a discussion of how to use the A3 can be found in the next section of this chapter) or a similar document that provides a description of the scope of the project, or "Scope Document." The document should, at a minimum, include the following:

1. The system being designed or redesigned
2. The principles that are guiding the design/redesign of the system
3. The ideal behaviors that the system should drive
4. The desired results that the behaviors should drive

A3 PROBLEM-SOLVING WORKSHEET

First you need to identify the project which will become the focus of your efforts. Document the project by identifying a champion for the project (someone who is willing to pay the bill) and form a team around the

Assessment Notes

AREA:	FOCUS:	ROUND:

IDEAL BEHAVIOR	OBSERVED BEHAVIOR
1	1
2	2
3	3
4	4
5	5
6	6
7	7
8	8
9	9
10	10

SYSTEMS	SYSTEM GENERATED BEHAVIORS

KEY QUESTIONS
1
2
3
4
5
6
7
8
9
10

FIGURE 11.3
Assessment Notes.

project. The qualitative methodology used when constructing the Impact/Effort Matrix should now be replaced with more quantitative values. The boss will want to know how much this will cost and how long it will take. He/she may also want you to spell out the benefits of doing this exercise. The tool for this is the A3 (Figure 11.4).

The purpose of the A3 is to show everything about the project on one sheet of paper. As shown in the chart, the A3 flows us through the project. It contains the following project steps:

1. Clarify and validate the problem (or opportunity) – What is the fundamental change you are trying to accomplish with this project? Give a description of the project in a couple of sentences.

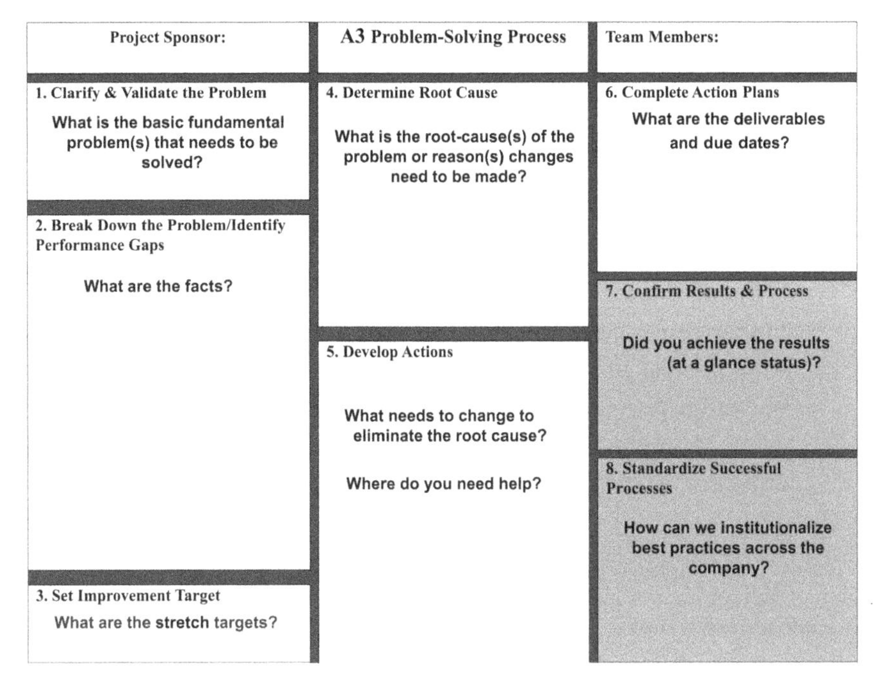

FIGURE 11.4
A3 Problem-Solving Worksheet.

2. Break down the problem and identify the performance gaps – This is where the numbers come in. What are the details that confirm the existence of the problem? Sometimes, when you consider a principle, numbers don't apply because the goal is to change the culture, and how does one quantify that? But even then, this is where one explains and justifies what it is they hope to accomplish with this change.
3. Set improvement targets – What is the goal that you are attempting to achieve by going through this change?
4. Determine the root cause – If it is a problem that one is trying to fix, what is the root cause of the problem? If it is an improvement that one is focused on, what is it that is not working as well as it should? Tools like the 5 Whys are valuable in this exercise.
5. Develop actions – Create a step-by-step list of activities that need to be completed to implement this change. This is also the point where you specify what resources are needed in order to accomplish the change, whether its money, or people, or time.

6. Complete action plans – Take the list from step 5 and put a timeline on it, including a specific list of all the deliverables you are planning to accomplish. At this point, all the steps necessary to get project approval should have been completed.
7. Confirm results and process – This is the section where we record (1) progress to the timeline, (2) show the deliverables listed in step 6, and (3) show that the target values listed in step 3 have been accomplished (or not).
8. Standardize successful process – Turn the new accomplishments to the process into standard work and share the learnings (both in the change process and in the changed process) with other relevant groups throughout the enterprise. Institutionalize this best practice across the company.

ROUND TWO

At this point, the team should have completed their "Go and Observe" Gemba exercise and should reconvene being ready to share the information that they learned with each other (this is referred to as a "go and do" exercise). This is an important part of the process. No idea should be suppressed, and "out of the box" thinking should be encouraged. This is a time for challenging questions like:

- Are we working on the correct system?
- Are we making the correct behavior–systems connections?
- Should the existing system be thrown out?
- Are there too many controls which are hampering the correct behaviors rather than magnifying them?
- Are we making the "right" thing (behaviors) easier to do than the "wrong" thing?
- And so on.

After a thorough discussion of the systems and behaviors that you are studying ("go and do" exercise), it is now time to redo the sheets in Chapters 9 and 10, reviewing everything and then preparing to return to the area that we are studying. It is time to repeat the "Go and Observe" exercise; this time drilling even deeper into the systems and behaviors being observed.

In this book, we will only be discussing two iterations of the "Go and Observe" each time, followed by the "go and do" exercise, but it is important to note that two is not a magic number. It may take five or even ten iterations before we truly understand what is going on. What is important is that we understand the system thoroughly, including its interactions with other systems, before we start making changes that can chain react in a negative way throughout the organization.

With each iteration, the objective of the "go and do" is for the teams to design/redesign a system to change behaviors so that the behaviors are closer to the ideal behaviors as measured by the appropriate KBIs. These KBIs should lead to improved results (KPIs).

After the "go and do," the teams should now revisit the designated locations and continue work on the designated system. The deliverable at the end of the exercise should again be an A3 or similar document. At this point, we need to provide a plan of action for the implementation of the project, or "Implementation Plan" which can be incorporated as part of the A3 (Figure 11.4). This document should, at a minimum, include the following:

1. A breakdown of the different steps of the plan
2. A time schedule for the implementation of each of the steps
3. The person, or people, responsible for each step
4. The plan for measuring results – including metrics and how those metrics will be measured

It is important for you to ask yourself the following questions as a review of your efforts. These are big picture questions designed to make sure you did not lose focus on what you were attempting to accomplish:

1. Which principles are exemplified via systems within your organization? What systems are driving specific behaviors?
2. Does your organization demonstrate "Building the Flow to Excellence?"
   - Where?
   - How?

PROJECT APPROVAL

At this point, we are assuming that you and your team have completed a thorough study of the behavioral issues and their associated systems. We are also assuming that you came up with a recommended solution, which includes some systems replacements or modifications. The next step in the process is to get funding and approval for the proposed changes. This requires a "go and do" team visit and a presentation of the A3 information to the appropriate system and/or area ownership and the person that holds the check book. The A3 that is brought into this meeting should include an implementation plan which contains the following information:

a. Be prepared to justify the system and changes you selected
b. Use the A3 format for the development of the plan
c. Offer a "straw man" plan of execution that will need to be vetted during the "Go and Observe" with executives
   - What are the steps in the plan?
   - What resources will be required to execute the plan?
   - What is the timeline for execution?
   - Who is responsible for each step?
   - What is the payback/reward/outcome by doing this execution?

SUMMARY

The purpose of this chapter was to "bring home" the process discussed throughout this book. Using this chapter, the reader should be able to assemble a project plan which modifies systems and their associated behaviors to get them closer to the ideal behaviors, get approval on that plan, and then move forward with the implementation of that plan. You should be well on your way toward creating a continuous improvement enterprise that strives toward excellence.

> Our scientific power has outrun our spiritual power. We have guided missiles and misguided men.
>
> **Martin Luther King, Jr**

12

Maintaining the Momentum

It is impossible to improve any process until it is standardized. If the process is shifting from here to there than any improvement will just be one more variation that is occasionally used and mostly ignored. One must standardize the process before improvements can be made.

Masaaki Imai

WE CAN'T STOP REFLECTING

The space program and NASA have shifted their focus, and there is a lot of confusion in the aerospace industry attempting to determine what they should work on next. The United States is using foreign rockets to launch satellites, and private companies are fighting their way toward becoming the first commercial provider of space transportation including tourism.

Being tangled up in these struggles finds American aerospace companies in a quandary, attempting to redefine themselves. Companies that were once the primary industry in a community are now only supporting a small portion of the population.

The editor of this book was brought into a company of this type and was asked to help them redefine themselves. Unfortunately, the company was extremely silo-ed. The manufacturing silo was in direct conflict with the engineering silo. Engineering felt that the only way to save the company was by coming up with creative technologies, like lift mechanisms into space that did not require rockets or hypersonic speed engines. Manufacturing was looking for ways to make cheaper rockets and was not interested in wasting time producing engineering's fantasies.

The author of this book was involved in organizing an off-site strategy workshop where the leadership and senior management were brought together in the hope that a unified plan could be created. It was a disaster because it turned into a power struggle between the various factions of the organization. In the end, they came up with a vision and strategy that cemented conflict between the divisions. The company's leadership was not forceful enough in their commitment to create a vision that the entire company could stand behind. They let the engineering and manufacturing organizations run over them. After this strategy workshop, the editor refused to work with them any longer. Since then, the company has seen major declines in their revenues, and they are on the verge of bankruptcy. A strong commitment to Enterprise Excellence success starts with leadership, and without it, there is no moving forward.

MOVING FORWARD

At this point, you should be ready to move forward, working your way up the ladder to sustainable Enterprise Excellence. Let us take a quick peek into the future. What do we need to do in order to maintain the momentum on a long-term basis? How do we maintain/sustain the progress we have made? How do we maintain the cycle of getting better and better?

To answer these questions, we need to start by reviewing the roles of leaders and managers in increasing or accelerating the momentum. Figure 12.1 reminds us that in order to create the desired cultural transformation, we need to take a close look at who creates the culture and what roles each of the enterprises' employees have in creating that culture. To do that, we will arbitrarily break the enterprises' employees up into three groups: leaders (CEO and VP levels, corporate executives, BoD, president – those who have responsibility over a group of managers and associates and provide strategic direction for the organization), managers (middle management – those who have responsibility over a group of associates and have tactical responsibility for the execution of the strategy), and associates (supervisors and shop floor employees – those who work under the direction of a manager and have responsibility for the work that they perform). In general, leaders create the culture. Managers make sure systems (which influence behaviors) are aligned to the culture. And

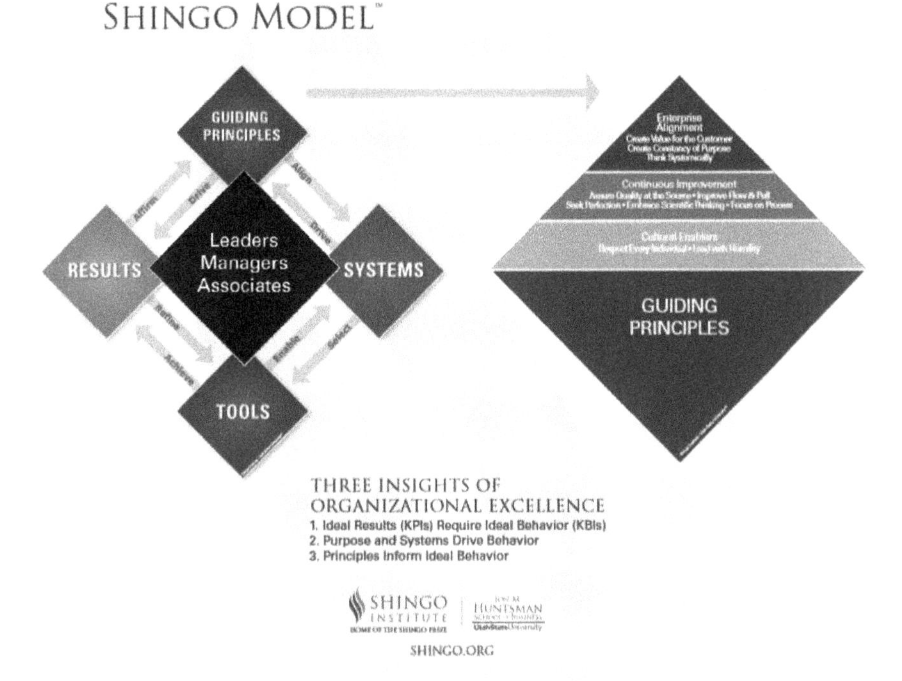

FIGURE 12.1
Leader Focus.

associates are mostly focused on the tools and are influenced by the culture. They learn how to work with or work around cultural limitations.

When you look at the model in Figure 12.1, leaders typically focus the most on "Results." They accomplish this by creating better systems that drive the enterprise toward improved results (for a more detailed discussion of the roles of leaders, managers, and associates, refer to the *Discover Excellence* book which spends a couple of chapters discussing these roles).

Figure 12.2 is another Shingo graphic first introduced in the Discover Excellence course, which shows what proportion of their time each of the three roles plays at each level of the Shingo Model. The breakdown is as follows:

Guiding Principles – Leaders spend 80 % of their time
Results and Systems – Managers spend 80 % of their time
Tools – Associates spend 80 % of their time

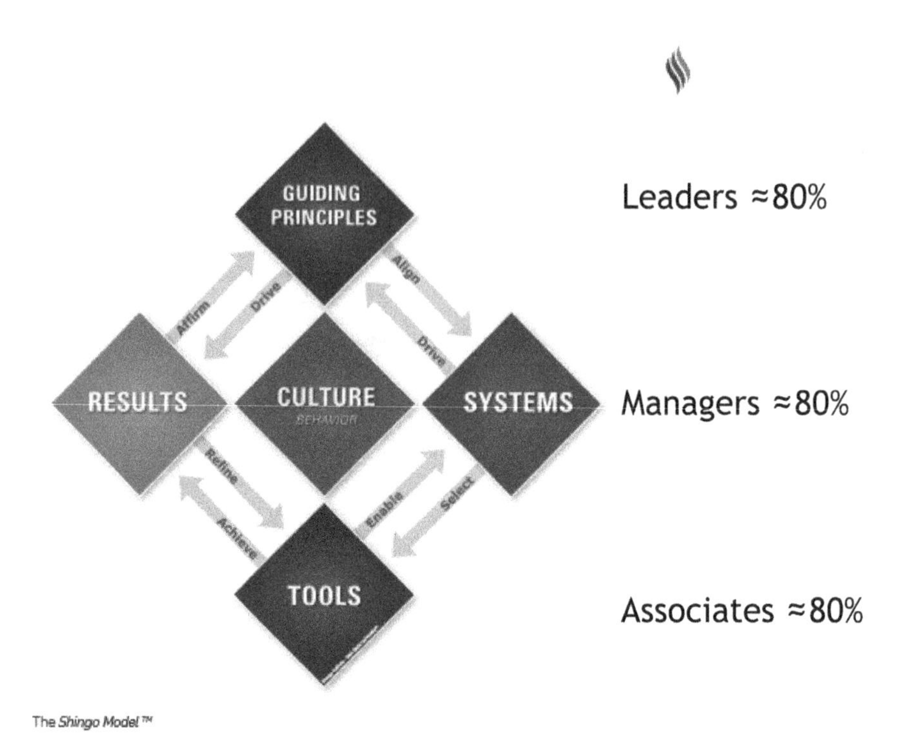

FIGURE 12.2
Areas of Focus.

With these approximations, we needed to ask the question, "Does ideal behavior vary by role?" The answer, of course, is "no" since ideal behaviors are universal. In the earlier workshop, we learned that culture starts at the top with leaders modeling ideal behaviors. Until the organization's employees are able to witness a commitment to ideal behaviors at the leadership level, they won't make the shift to Shingo Principles. As part of this process, leadership needs to make sure that there are not any legacy systems that conflict or contradict the principle-focused systems we are trying to exemplify. Eliminate systems that cause conflict and replace them with systems that support ideal behaviors.

Utilizing the third and last slide from the Discover Excellence workshop, we look at the section where this workshop discussed the roles of leaders, managers, and associates. In Figure 12.3, we show one of the many examples that were presented, where we are tying a principle with the specific roles of leaders, managers, and associates, with respect to that

Principle:	Respect Every Individual
Leaders:	Leaders always acknowledge the specific behaviors they see that are close to ideal
Managers:	Every manager makes certain that large group meetings begin with a safety briefing.
Associates:	Associates demonstrate an eagerness to learn new skills, take initiative, and share their learning and success with others

Systems:	Recognition Safety Communication
Tools:	Recognition events & appreciation cards Proper safety equipment Newsletter

FIGURE 12.3
Ideal Behaviors.

principle, and the types of systems and tools that are often linked to that principle.

As leaders and managers, we need to repeatedly ask ourselves questions about our roles and responsibilities with respect to each of the principles that we will be focusing on. For example:

- What is the definition of our roles and responsibilities with respect to this principle? Are they performing the right roles?
- What is our cadence for meeting and tracking progress on improvements with respect to each principle? Do we have a governance system established? Regular reviews, either monthly or quarterly, depending on the amount of focus that is being placed on the principle under consideration, are critical.
- How have systems been adjusted to support the ideal behaviors that we are looking for? Who has ownership of these changes? Who is working to adjust these systems?

The key to all of this is governance. We cannot just make a fix and assume that it will last forever on its own volition. A philosophy of "review and report" is necessary for several reasons:

- It makes us accountable
- It keeps everyone informed about the progress of change
- It teaches others and motivates others toward improvements

We strongly recommend a standardized format for the report-outs. Our recommendation is to use the A3 format that you were introduced to in the last chapter. The reason for using the A3 is that it is concise, restricted to one page, and that everyone becomes familiar with a standard format which, over time, will make it a lot easier for the organization to use.

MAINTAINING THE MOMENTUM

Figure 12.4 shows John Kotter's eight steps for maintaining the momentum for change. The Shingo Institute does not necessarily endorse this model, but it is a good one for us to consider. Some model or methodology for change should be considered by your organization.

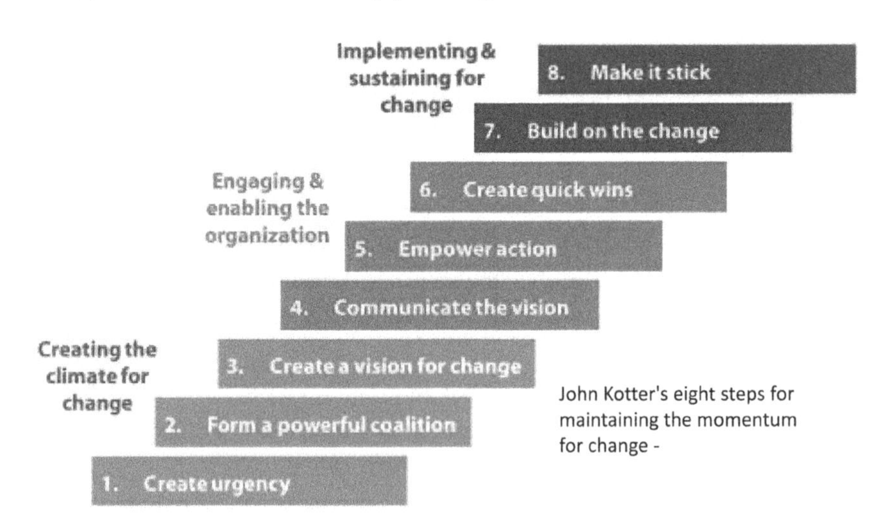

FIGURE 12.4
Maintaining Momentum.

In Kotter's model, we see three stages of change:

A. Creating the climate for change
B. Engaging and enabling the organization
C. Implementing and sustaining for change

Most organizations struggle with the first of these three stages, considering it the hardest to overcome. In this first stage, the model has three steps:

1. Create urgency – The struggle with this first step is that leadership and management must first feel the urgency before the rest of the organization can follow. In our experience, we have often found that leadership supports and identifies a need for change, but that middle management resists that urgency. Management tends to prefer stability. Their job becomes more difficult and often feels threatened when change is introduced. It is not unusual to find companies where large portions of middle management leave the organization, either voluntarily or by force, because they refused to follow leaderships' desire to change. Hence, unless both leadership and management are united in the urgency to change, it will not happen.
2. Form a powerful coalition – The coalition that we create needs to incorporate all three levels of the organization. At first, the coalition requires the unified support of leadership and management. Then, we need to introduce the organization's associates into the coalition. Not everyone will be on board immediately. But over time, after parts of the organization have demonstrated successes, growing the coalition to be organization-wide becomes easier and easier.
3. Create a vision for change – This step does not suggest that leadership wait with their vision for change. They should already have this vision in their mind. However, what this step suggests is that the organization as a whole needs to become absorbed in this vision and needs to incorporate it into their daily thinking habits.

The second of these three stages, engaging and enabling the organization, becomes easier if the first stage has been fully executed. In this second stage, the model again has three steps:

4. Communicate the vision – One of the failures of most organizations is that the leadership gets together once a year, creates a corporate vision, posts it on the wall, and then forgets about it for the rest of

the year. The success or failure of this process is easy to test. Just call a meeting of the leadership and ask them to write down the corporate vision. Rarely does anyone get it right. If this is true about the corporate vision, what chance does the "vision for change" have in being remembered throughout the organization? Communicating the vision requires constantly bringing the message to the forefront of every meeting, constantly holding everyone accountable for the changes that they are involved in and requiring employees to search for change opportunities.

5. Empower action – This principle is also found in the Shingo Principles. It basically says that we need to give the power to make changes to those individuals who are the most familiar with the process being changed. We cannot require leadership approval for every change, or it will never happen. The power to change needs to be with the associates.
6. Create quick wins – Quick wins work as a motivation tool and as a sales tool, facilitating buy-in into the change process. They also fast-track us to receiving some benefits as quickly as possible. Why not gain benefits as quickly as possible? If there are some easy wins, let us do them as soon as possible. Quick wins are highlighted in the Impact/Effort Matrix that we discussed earlier by being in the upper left-hand quadrant of the diagram (Figure 11.1).

The third of these three stages, implementing and sustaining for change, is the area of continuous change that we are trying to emphasize in this chapter. However, we need to consider all the steps in the model in order for this last stage to be successful. In this last stage, we emphasize the sharing, growing, and governance that supports a well-constructed change management structure.

7. Build on the change – Governance and report-outs become a critical tool for sharing successes. The more other parts of the organization see success within the organization, the more they become interested and engaged in achieving their own successes. This step also suggests that just because we have made a change doesn't mean we are finished. The philosophy of "continuous improvement" requires

us to look for ways to additionally improve even those things that we have already improved.
8. Make it stick – This is where we focus on sustainable continuous improvement excellence, which is the goal and objective of the Shingo methodology and this book. The focus is on a cultural shift throughout the organization which has all levels of the organization go through a mental transformation, where, in the end, they worked together on a unified vision toward achieving Enterprise Excellence.

Using this change model as an example, we can see how a structured approach is necessary in order to achieve our Enterprise Excellence goals.

FEEDBACK

The reader of this book, or the attendee of any of the Shingo workshops, has not completed their effort unless they share their learnings with their leadership. You need to provide leadership feedback. We recommend the following types of information to be relayed:

- What behavioral benchmarks were observed during the "Go and Observe"? What benchmarks were missing? What else needs to be worked on?
- What were the ideal behaviors and systems studied? What systems' transformations are needed? Your thoughts and recommendations are critical here.
- Your observations/recommendations beyond just looking at systems and benchmarks are needed. For example, is standard work universally applied? Is the corporate vision universally understood? Is the management receptive to change?
- Also important are any additional observed 5S concerns like, safety. With leadership, management, and associate permission, we have often videotaped portions of processes in order to study the process and have found enormous safety failures that leadership and management had no idea were happening. This is not tattletaling.

This is caring about the safety and welfare of the employees, and if management does not know about the problem, they can't fix it.

SUMMARY

This chapter has discussed sustainability. Ultimately, without sustainability, the improvements that have been made tend to slowly melt away and tradition creeps back in, thereby labeling this continuous improvement process a failure. However, with a sustained continuous improvement process, your organization, just like the many others we have discussed, can become one of the many "Enterprise Excellent" organizations.

> Modern Man's seven social sins
> wealth without work
> pleasure without conscience
> knowledge without character
> commerce without morality
> science without humanity
> religion without sacrifice, and
> politics without principle
>
> **Mahatma Gandhi**

13

Sustainable Enterprise Excellence

Rather than merely telling people to work better, it is much more productive to set out clear objectives and to provide motivation.

Shigeo Shingo

ARE WE WINNING?

Let us define winning. To win means that you are better today than you were yesterday. Better at what? Better at your KBIs. Better at your KPIs. Closer to having an enterprise excellent culture focused on continuous improvement. Toyota leadership has expressed the concern that when you become number one, you tend to become lax in your efforts to improve. For that reason, it is better to not become number one. Their way around this is to compare yourself with yourself and to demonstrate continuous improvements. You can read about this Toyota way of thinking in the new book *Toyota's Global Marketing Strategy: Innovation through Breakthrough Thinking and Kaizen*, Taylor and Francis Group, CRC Press, 2017, with authors Hibino, Noguchi, and Plenert.

We are winning if we are moving closer to our vision and strategy through the culture-based improvement process outlined by the Shingo Institute and as described in this book and the six Shingo workshops.

LEARNING OBJECTIVES

Before we close out this book, let us review the objectives of this book and make sure we achieved them all.

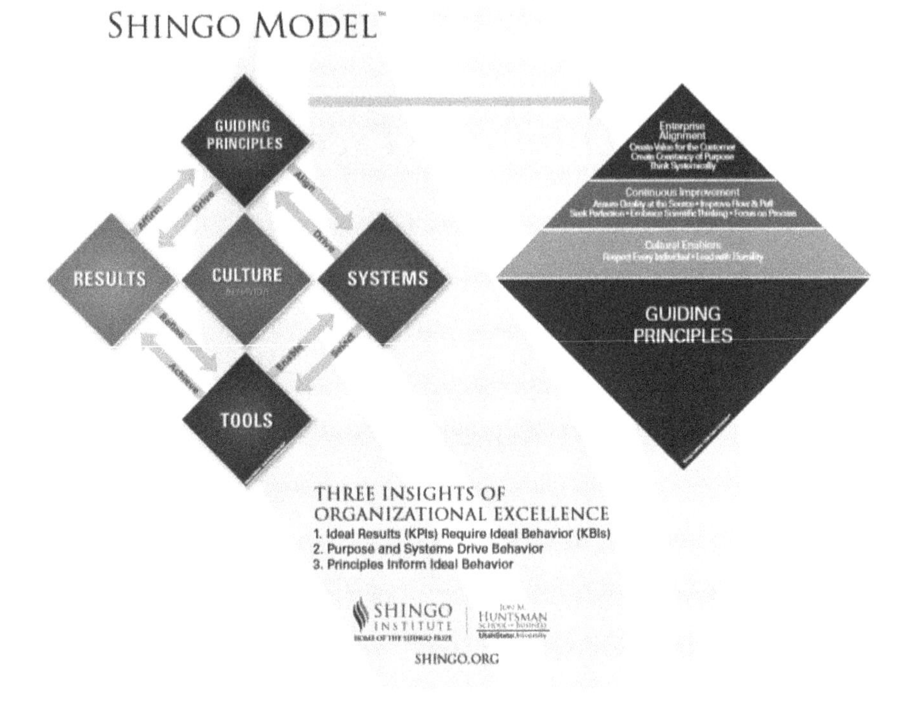

FIGURE 13.1
The Shingo Model.

1. Understand the Shingo Model and how it builds cultural transformation with a goal of creating an environment of sustainable continuous improvement (Figure 13.1).
2. Show how individual objectives drive toward the organizational objectives.
3. Answer the question, "How do I influence leadership and get everyone on board?"
4. Build on the principles of Enterprise Excellence.
5. Understand the relationship between behaviors, systems, and principles and how they drive to results.
6. Learn how KBIs drive KPIs and how this leads to excellent results.
7. Use "Go and Observe" to understand the practical application of the *Shingo Guiding Principles*.

These objectives have been met in the various chapters throughout this book. But that does not mean that we should close this book and never

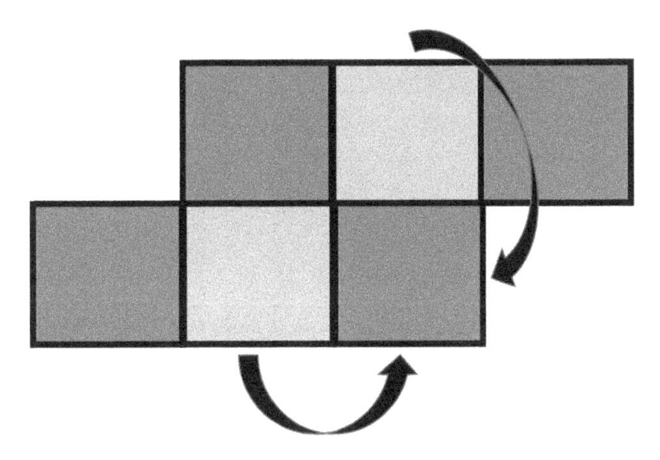

FIGURE 13.2
The Solution.

look at it again. Rather, this book should become a reference book that you refer to on a regular basis as you go through your organizational transformations. It should become worn out long before you achieve Enterprise Excellence.

Before we conclude this chapter, there is one last item of business that needs to be resolved. In the preface of this book, we were introduced to a puzzle. I am sure you were able to successfully resolve the puzzle, but for all your friends who weren't quite as clever, the answer is found in Figure 13.2.

Thank you for taking this Shingo journey with me. I am excited to see the transformation that will be occurring within your organization. Please keep me informed as you progress, and please feel free to contact me with any questions.

Gerhard Plenert, PhD, PO Box 267, La Verkin, UT 84745
gerhard@gerhardplenert.com

Insecure managers create complexity. Real leaders don't need clutter.

John F Welch, Jr
Chairman and CEO, General Electric

Index

Note: Page numbers followed by "*f*" refer to figures.

D

E

F

G

Q

R

S

T

U

V

W